Wicked INDIANAPOLIS

Wicked
INDIANAPOLIS

ANDREW E. STONER

Charleston · London

THE
History
PRESS

Published by The History Press
Charleston, SC 29403
www.historypress.net
Copyright © 2011 by Andrew E. Stoner
All rights reserved

Cover images: Front: Vice President Charles Warren Fairbanks; Western Union messenger
boys at Monument Circle, circa 1908; above buildings (left to right) are U.S. Senator
William D. Bynum, Mary Scott Lord Harrison and Caroline Scott Harrison. Back:
U.S. Senator and former governor Samuel M. Ralston, circa 1922; President Theodore
Roosevelt and Charles Warren Fairbanks at Roosevelt's home, July 16, 1904; the 1913
Indianapolis 500. All cover images are from the Library of Congress. All contemporary
images were contributed by photographer Steve Polston.

First published 2011
Manufactured in the United States
ISBN 978.1.60949.205.2
Stoner, Andrew E.
Wicked Indianapolis / Andrew E. Stoner.
p. cm.
Includes bibliographical references.
ISBN 978-1-60949-205-2
1. Indianapolis (Ind.)--History--Anecdotes. 2. Indianapolis (Ind.)--Biography--Anecdotes. 3.
Indianapolis (Ind.)--Social conditions--Anecdotes. 4. Indianapolis (Ind.)--Moral conditions-
-Anecdotes. 5. Crime--Indiana--Indianapolis--History--Anecdotes. 6. Corruption--
Indiana--Indianapolis--History--Anecdotes. 7. Scandals--Indiana--Indianapolis--History--
Anecdotes. I. Title.
F534.I357S86 2011
977.2'52--dc22
2011016280

For Randolph E. Scott.

Contents

Introduction   9

Part I: Infamous Celebrities

Plane Crash Claims Hoosier Film Legend Carole Lombard   11

Dr. Kinsey's Battle Line: Indianapolis   14

Ray Charles's Private Struggle Goes Public   17

Frances Farmer Presents   19

A Native Son Goes Terribly Awry   21

Elvis and Michael Invade Indy   24

The State of Indiana v. Mike Tyson   28

Chris Farley "Milks" Indy for Some of His Last Laughs   31

Part II: Infamous Criminals

John Dillinger on His Home Turf   35

The Art of the Deal Goes Deadly Wrong   37

Tony Kiritsis: Mad as Hell and Not Going to Take It Anymore   39

The Speedway Bomber   42

The "Yogurt Connection"   47

The Kmart Bombing Leads to Healing, Forgiveness   50

Indianapolis Vice   54

CONTENTS

Part III: Infamous Disasters

Train Disasters Have Left Their Mark 61

"Little Heroes of the Street" 66

Devastating Fires Seared into Indy's History 69

The "Great Pandemic of 1918" Claimed 1,632 Indy Lives 75

Fort Harrison's Deadly History 77

The Greatest Spectacle in Tragedy? 80

The Final Act: A Deadly Blast Kills Seventy-four 83

The Lethal Skies Above Indy 86

Part IV: Infamous Politicians

Hoosier Congressmen in the Hot Seat 95

Cleveland and Hendricks: A Short-Lived "Partnership" 98

Mr. Harrison Takes a Bride 100

Vice President "Cocktail Charlie" Warren Fairbanks 104

A Rough-and-Tumble Start for a "True Statesman" 108

Riot-Buster Ralston 110

A New Disclosure from Senator New 112

Make Room in the Jail for a Mayor and a Governor 115

Jesse L. Dickinson Overcomes Jim Crow 118

George Wallace's Northern Encroachment 120

A Hoosier Not to Be Confused with the Facts 123

The Butz of a Bad Joke 124

Negley's Negligence 126

Dan Quayle's "Excellent Adventure" 127

A Scandal Worth Betting On 131

A Footnote in Indiana Politics: Dwayne M. Brown 134

Dan Burton's Glass House Shatters 137

Notes 141

Bibliography 153

About the Author 159

Introduction

E very major American city can lay claim to—or attempt to deny—any number of scandals or homegrown scoundrels or even disasters that people would rather forget. Indianapolis is no different. As the capital of Indiana, it's been more than the "Crossroads of America"—it's also been the crossroads of incredible incidents of happenstance and planning.

Contained here are some of the stories you won't find in the state's history books—stories left out of the fourth-grade Indiana history curriculum required of all Hoosier schoolchildren. But love it or hate it, these stories are also an important part of the amalgam that is Indiana at the heart of the nation.

In telling some of the most incredible stories in Indianapolis history, we learn more about ourselves and our values. When we look at political scandal, major disasters, criminal activity and the role celebrities play in our culture, we gain a greater sense of what it means to be Hoosier. As a people, we don't tolerate scandal, scoundrels or criminals. We often watch with a sense of curiosity what the celebrities who come through Indianapolis impart. Most of all, we gather up our best efforts and respond with compassion and action when disaster strikes.

As you read this story of Indianapolis, written by someone who has grown to love the Circle City, refresh your memory of some of the "big events" that came along. And don't share this book with outsiders. They'll never understand.

To learn more about major Indianapolis events such as the LaSalle Street murders and the Sylvia Likens case, or about a variety of other major crimes, see Historic Indianapolis Crimes: Murder and Mystery in the Circle City, *another History Press title by Fred D. Cavinder.*

Part I
Infamous Celebrities

PLANE CRASH CLAIMS HOOSIER FILM LEGEND CAROLE LOMBARD

The Friday morning, January 16, 1942 edition of the *Indianapolis Star* carried a four-column picture of Hollywood legend Carole Lombard (1908–1942) posing for a photo with Indiana governor Henry F. Schricker (1883–1966) and Indianapolis mayor Reginald H. Sullivan (1876–1980) as the U.S. flag was raised to start a war bonds rally on the east steps of the Indiana Statehouse.

It was one of the last stops on her whirlwind visit to her home state, resulting in more than $2 million in sales of American war bonds and stamps to support efforts to win World War II. Lombard's effort set a single-day bond sale record and easily surpassed the campaign's goal of $500,000. She personally signed autographs for each bond purchased and later told a downtown Indianapolis crowd, "This has been a wonderful, memorable day. Nothing could have made me happier than your kind invitation to share it with you and to be in Indianapolis tonight."[1]

Hoosiers were rightfully enamored of Lombard, a Fort Wayne native. Only thirty-two years old, she was already a major film star and the wife of fellow film legend Clark Gable (1901–1960), reportedly earning a $465,000-per-year salary from MGM—a massive sum in the 1940s.

Lombard and her mother, Elizabeth Peters (1877–1942), had taken a three-day train ride to get to Indiana from Los Angeles, but Carole longed for a quicker return trip. It meant boarding a TWA luxury liner just after 5:00 a.m. at the Indianapolis airport. There she signed her last known autograph ever in Indianapolis to a Howe High School student—as "Carole Lombard Gable."

Lombard wanted to get home to see Gable, saying that she had never been away from him for longer than three days. Gable's personal MGM publicity agent, Otto W. Winkler (1903–1942), flipped a coin to solve a disagreement between Lombard and her mother about whether to take the plane (or a train, as favored by Mrs. Peters).

TWA Flight 3, which would carry the party from Indianapolis, had originated in New York and was scheduled for several stops, including Albuquerque, New Mexico, and Boulder, Colorado, before arriving in Los Angeles. No direct flights were available, but Lombard was not to be deterred. The TWA liner was not a sleeping flight, but Lombard told reporters that she didn't mind. "When I get home, I'll flop in bed and sleep for 12 hours," she said, smiling.[2]

The flight ran behind schedule all day, however, and the TWA pilot changed plans and replaced Boulder (an airport with no nighttime runway lights) with Las Vegas. In Albuquerque, media reports indicated that twelve army crewmen and one civilian boarded the plane. The trip to Vegas's airport was uneventful, and the plane landed there at about 6:36 p.m. and added fuel. The plane departed the Las Vegas airport at 7:07 p.m. local time.

By 7:20 p.m., the plane had lost radio contact with the Las Vegas tower. At almost 7:23 p.m., workers at the Blue Diamond Mine reported that they "saw a flare, then heard an explosion" about thirty miles southwest of the city.

"The plane, traveling at more than 150 miles per hour, had slammed into the top of Mount Potosi [also known as Olcott or Table Rock Mountain]… the plane had failed to clear the mountaintop by fewer than 60 feet. The gasoline tank, located under the passengers, exploded," recounted author Robert D. McCracken in his book *Las Vegas: The Great American Playground*.[3]

Media reports indicated that Gable rushed from Los Angeles to Las Vegas via another flight, "had to be dissuaded from attempting to climb to the crash site" and ultimately remained secluded at a Las Vegas hotel, "described as badly broken up." Fellow actor Spencer Tracy (1900–1967) traveled with Gable and consoled him.[4]

Gable and other family members of the twenty-one passengers on board (in addition to Lombard) waited all day Saturday and into Sunday until posses returned from the area with the grim news: there were no survivors; the plane and everyone on board had died of blunt-force injuries or had burned to death.

Gable apparently felt great responsibility for Lombard's death, having declined to go on the war bond trip and agreeing with her suggestion that she go instead. One searcher reportedly gave Gable a damaged diamond and ruby clip, a treasured piece that the actor kept with him the rest of his life.[5]

While he couldn't help locate the bodies, Gable did accompany the body of his beloved (and third) wife and her mother on a train from Las Vegas to Los Angeles. Consistent with her wishes, Gable ensured that she was buried in a small, private ceremony inside a mausoleum at Forest Lawn Cemetery in Hollywood. Gable purchased three crypts, one each for Carole and her mother and one for himself (in which he was laid to rest upon his death in 1960).

Lombard's death shook the normally cynical Hollywood—she was, after all, among the small but elite group of actors who had made the transition from silent movies to "talkies." "The tragedy of Carole Lombard, girl of the hard-boiled chatter and the tender heart, in the fiery wreckage of transport plane saddened the sound stages today and caused many a fellow performer to weep," one Hollywood dispatch reported. "No other current actress was so universally beloved: the death of no other glamour girl since Jean Harlow had such a profound effect as this news on the movie makers, sentimentalists all."[6]

Hollywood writer Hubbard Keavy said, "Carole had a masculine deliberateness about her career. She always was sure of herself, but if a role turned out badly, she never shifted the blame, as is the Hollywood custom. She would say, in characteristic fashion, 'I sure stunk up that one.'"[7]

President Franklin D. Roosevelt (1882–1945) and First Lady Eleanor Roosevelt (1884–1962) wired Gable with their condolences. "Mrs. Roosevelt and I are deeply distressed," the president's cable noted. "Carole was our friend, our guest in happier days. She brought great joy to all who knew her and to the millions who knew her only as a great artist. She gave unselfishly of time and talent to serve her government in peace and in war. She loved her country."[8]

A Federal Bureau of Investigation (FBI) inquiry into the crash—in the years before the Federal Aviation Administration conducted such probes—ruled the cause of the flight to be pilot error. It concluded that the pilot had failed to alter his flight plan from the original Boulder route and, as a result, did not account properly for the mountains surrounding the Las Vegas area.

In her career, Lombard starred in fifty-seven separate films between 1921 and 1942. "Even five decades later, *Entertainment Weekly* magazine called the thirty-three year old actress' death 'one of the damndest shames in movie history,'" wrote Indiana historian Nelson Price.[9]

DR. KINSEY'S BATTLE LINE: INDIANAPOLIS

On March 23, 1957, the Anderson Police Department notified the FBI field office in Indianapolis that it had seized "25 reels of 8 mm and 15 reels of 16 mm obscene films, playing cards, books and pamphlets, also of an obscene nature."[10]

The items were taken from "two tool boxes which a cab driver had been given $10 to obtain from the Pennsylvania Railroad Station lockers...after which he was to express them as designated to the Research Institute at Indiana University."[11] The cab driver, growing suspicious of his instructions, flagged down an Anderson police officer, and the materials—intended for the growing collection of erotica at the Indiana University (IU) Institute for Sexual Research—were confiscated, after which empty boxes were sent on to Bloomington.[12]

It was just the latest run-in that the institute would experience as it attempted to become an international research source on human sexuality—with Alfred C. Kinsey (1894–1956), a zoology and biology professor at IU, leading the charge.

Not only did the customs battle in Indianapolis prove to be a turning point for Kinsey and IU, the city had also provided rich texture for the sexuality studies undertaken already. Before moving on to Chicago and other large cities, Kinsey and his colleagues spent considerable time taking "sexual histories" from prostitutes and gay men and women in Indianapolis, including at the Indiana Women's Prison.[13]

Kinsey's research would gain worldwide attention—both with his 1948 publication of *Sexual Behavior in the Human Male* and with the following *Sexual Behavior in the Human Female* in 1953. In subsequent years, scholarly researchers and historians raised serious questions about the methods and validity of Kinsey's qualitative/quantitative approaches; Kinsey's fame in the 1950s was so great that it brought him intense scrutiny.

Initially benefiting from a "gentleman's agreement" with customs officials in Indianapolis, a key Kinsey contact in the U.S. Customs Office in Indianapolis was on vacation when another shipment of erotica came through. His replacement deemed the materials obscene and set off an elaborate seven-year battle between Kinsey (and ultimately Indiana University) and the federal government.

"For the past six years, federal customs sleuths have been impounding, as fast as it poured into the U.S. from Europe and the Orient, a vast collection of erotica consigned to the Institute for Sex Research of Indiana University's Sexpatiator Alfred C. Kinsey," reported *Time* magazine. "The government last week gave Zoologist Kinsey and his sexociates until this month's end to show why the treasure-trove of pornography should not be destroyed."[14]

Kinsey told reporters, "The issue involved is the right of a scholar to have access to material which is denied the general public."[15]

Kinsey had a powerful backer in his efforts—famed IU president Herman B Wells (1902–2000). Wells wrote in his 1980 autobiography that "[i]t is difficult now to make vivid the steady national uproar over a number of years as the Kinsey studies unfolded" and added:

> *When we were unable to get the federal government to release the materials for the institute's library that had been impounded by Customs in Indianapolis, it became necessary to bring suit against the government. The Board of Trustees took the extraordinary action of volunteering to hire outstanding counsel for the university to appeal with the Kinsey Institute...In my judgment, the trustees' action in this instance is among the proudest moments in the annals of the Indiana University Board of Trustees and in the history of Indiana University. I am now convinced that the importance that we attached to the defense of the Kinsey Institute was not exaggerated. Time has proven that the defense was important, not only for the understanding of sexual activity, but also for the welfare of the university. It reinforced the faculty's sense of freedom to carry on their work without fear of interference, and it established in the public mind that the university had an integrity that could not be bought, pressured or subverted.*[16]

A close associate of Kinsey's, Wardell B. Pomeroy (1913–2001), noted that their work was often complicated by "gossip fed by the *Indianapolis Star*, a right-wing organ which lost no opportunity to put Kinsey in a bad light, no matter what the facts might be." Poor press relations boiled over in Indianapolis when Kinsey attempted to keep reporters out of an October 1956 speech that he had planned before psychiatrists meeting in Indianapolis.[17]

Pomeroy and Paul H. Gebhard (who succeeded Kinsey as head of the institute after Kinsey's untimely death in 1956) would figure prominently in ongoing battles with the FBI and customs officials.

Documents released by the FBI in recent years show that it was adamant about keeping a close eye on the institute. Following the Anderson, Indiana snafu, the FBI's field office in Indianapolis attempted to get Pomeroy and Gebhard to release the names of individuals who had sent them "obscene" materials in the past—a request they refused. Turning the tables on the feds, Pomeroy filed a request with the FBI to inspect *its* seized records of

FBI director J. Edgar Hoover, circa 1940. *Library of Congress LC-H22-D-8745.*

so-called obscene materials—a request that drew a handwritten response directly from the FBI's powerful director, J. Edgar Hoover (1895–1972), "In so far as any material FBI has, it is NOT going to be made available to this outfit."[18]

Indiana University and the Kinsey Institute eventually won the legal battle with customs officials, settled in 1958, two years after Kinsey's death. Today, the so-called Kinsey Collection contains more than fourteen thousand erotic films and video tapes and thousands more pieces of erotic art and sex items from around the world.[19]

Ray Charles's Private Struggle Goes Public

The early 1960s was an exciting time in the ultimately incredible career of American singer Ray Charles (1930–2004), whose full name was Ray Charles Robinson. Ranked by *Rolling Stone* magazine as one of the top one hundred musical performers of all time, Charles's songs were hitting the charts hard in the 1960s, and his concert tours brought him to Indiana in November 1961.

Born the son of a Georgia sharecropper, Charles began to lose his sight as a small boy and was completely blind from the age of seven. His blindness did nothing to dull his drive and talent, and he grew to become an accomplished gospel, jazz and soul pianist who scored major record hits. His biggest crossover hits included "The Night Time (Is The Right Time)," "What'd I Say," "Georgia On My Mind," "Hit the Road Jack" and "I Can't Stop Loving You."

Musical success, however, could not hide Charles's growing heroin addiction, one that landed him in jail in Indianapolis on November 13, 1961. Then just thirty-one years old, Charles was arrested in a room at the downtown Sheraton-Lincoln Hotel. Charles and his sixteen-piece band had lodged at Indy overnight after a performance at Anderson and en route to another performance at Evansville.

Indianapolis vice detectives said that they went to the hotel after they were told by another officer that Charles had narcotics with him. As the *Indianapolis News* reported, Detective Sergeant William Owen said that he "knocked on the door to Suite 717–719, and told a man who answered from behind the door that he was from Western Union. The detective said that when the door was opened, the man said he was Charles."[20]

Invited into the suite, according to Owen, he and his partner Robert Keithley then identified themselves as police officers and "searched the suite and found 13 tablets that later proved to contain traces of heroin. They also found needles and a syringe and Charles showed them a jar containing marijuana."[21]

The *Indianapolis Star* reported that Charles openly admitted to police that he had been "a drug addict for half his life" and had bought the heroin tablets in Indianapolis for three dollars apiece. Owen told reporters that Charles's "needle-marked arm was one of the worst I've ever seen." Charles did have one prior arrest, in 1958, for drug possession in Philadelphia.[22]

Charles was back in Indianapolis in January 1962 and asked a Marion County Municipal Court judge to dismiss the charges against him because the police had handled their investigation improperly. Eventually, the judge agreed, and Charles was released after having only served his initial arrest period before posting bail.

The *Indianapolis News* ran a sad front-page photo on the day of his hearing that showed a forlorn Charles seated in a chair outside the Indianapolis courtroom, obviously unaware that he was being photographed. Charles did not testify at the hearing.

His drug problems, however, were not behind him altogether. He was arrested again on October 31, 1964, after airport customs officers in Boston found heroin, marijuana and a syringe in his overcoat. Ultimately given a suspended sentence, in 1964 entertainment reports indicated that Charles was entering drug rehabilitation. He did not appear in public again until 1965, with the release of his cover version of the country song "Crying Time."

Sober and back on his game, Charles eventually earned twelve separate Grammy awards between 1960 and 1990 and appeared in ten films, including a memorable performance in the 1980 hit *The Blues Brothers*. Near the end of his career, he made numerous memorable TV performances, including singing the national anthem at the Republican National Convention and hosting NBC's *Saturday Night Live*.

FRANCES FARMER PRESENTS

Hollywood actress Frances Farmer (1913–1970) had no ties to Indianapolis except during the last years of her life, when she tried to secure at least some of the peace and happiness that had eluded her in her earlier life.

An accomplished stage and screen star, Farmer was a growing star in Hollywood, starring in sixteen films in the 1930s and 1940s alongside the likes of Bing Crosby (1903–1977), Cary Grant (1904–1986) and Tyrone Power (1914–1958).

Known for her handsome, daring good looks and fashion, Farmer is perhaps best known, however, for the struggle to regain her life. The 1982 film *Frances*, starring Jessica Lange and Kim Stanley, earned two Oscar nominations for its stars and introduced Farmer to a whole new generation of Americans who had long forgotten her. Farmer's family and others have refuted the film's major claims that the actress was subjected to painful electroshock treatments and a lobotomy against her will.

Farmer's troubles began, most believe, in October 1942 when she was arrested for failing to cooperate with an order from a Santa Monica, California police officer who had stopped her for driving with her headlights on. In America's coastal cities during World War II, "blackout" periods required that drivers abide by the low- or no-lights rule. Suspected of being drunk, Farmer's reportedly combative reaction to the police officer resulted in a night in jail, a fine and probation.

In January 1943, a bench warrant was issued for Farmer's arrest for failure to pay her fine. It appeared that her time away from the court had not mellowed her or removed her love of the drink. An incredible scene played out as Farmer wrestled with court guards and a jail matron—newspapers across the country showing embarrassing pictures of Farmer being dragged from the courtroom against her will—and was later pictured handcuffed and looking like a woman who had been in a fight.[23]

The judge ordered Farmer to be held for a mental health evaluation, and from there her life got very difficult. Helped by her family's insistence that they could not control her or curb her behavior—as well as the abandonment of her by her husband, agent and movie studios for being too much trouble—Farmer found herself committed to mental hospitals and sanitariums. It is here where controversy arises—the film *Frances* depicts all sorts of rudimentary and experimental "treatments" being tried on her, claims that others dispute.

Between 1943 and 1950, Farmer was in and out of mental health facilities, not regaining her emancipation from her family until a court order entered in 1953. By the late 1950s, she was making spotty appearances in regional theater and on two CBS dramatic series, *Playhouse 90* and *Westinghouse Presents Studio One*. She also scored two appearances on *The Ed Sullivan Show* and a profile on NBC's *This Is Your Life*.

Her network TV appearances did not win her major film roles, however, and she was recruited to come to Indianapolis's WFBM-TV, the local NBC affiliate, to host *Frances Farmer Presents*. The show consisted of Farmer introducing an afternoon matinee each day on WFBM and ran from 1958 to 1964.

Some friends said, after her death, that her years in Indianapolis were ones of peace and happiness for her. She joined the Catholic Church and reportedly enjoyed having a regular paycheck. They were not, however, years without reminders of Farmer's troubled past. WFBM officials fired Farmer just weeks after a disastrous publicity interview they had arranged

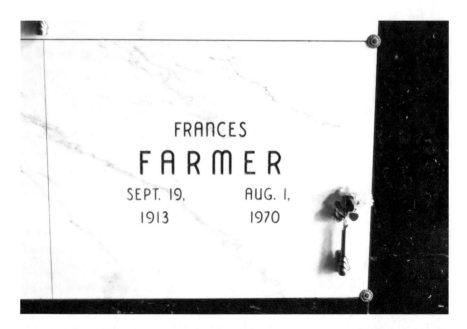

Grave site of Frances Farmer, Oaklawn Memorial Gardens. *Photo by Steve Polston.*

for her on NBC's *Today Show* in 1964 that seemingly focused almost entirely on her past problems.

Off TV and out of work, Farmer accepted roles on stage with the Drama Department at Purdue University in West Lafayette, Indiana. She was in the headlines again for an October 24, 1965 arrest by police near Lebanon, Indiana, who cited her for drunk driving as she drove back to her home in Indianapolis. The local justice of the peace fined Farmer $68.50 and suspended her driver's license for sixty days after an Indiana state trooper reported that "her auto had been weaving on and off the median of Interstate 65."[24]

Farmer stayed out of the headlines until her death at the age of fifty-six in August 1970 from esophageal cancer at Community Hospital in Indianapolis. Some reports since then indicated that her final years in the Circle City were ones of struggle; one report indicated she was reduced to collecting tin cans and bottles for cash. She is buried at Oak Lawn Memorial Gardens in Fishers, Indiana.[25]

A NATIVE SON GOES TERRIBLY AWRY

During his years in Indianapolis, Reverend Jim Jones (1931–1978) was a well-respected voice for Christians, Catholics and Jews who were concerned about issues of social justice in the slow-to-change city of Indianapolis.

Jones was so respected; in fact, that Indianapolis mayor Charles Boswell (1909–1976), a Democrat, appointed the young pastor to lead the city's newly formed Human Rights Commission at an annual salary of $7,000. Creation of the commission was a step forward for Indianapolis, but the mayor asked Jones to proceed carefully, knowing that it would take the city many years to overcome much of its racist heritage.

Jim Jones knew Indianapolis well. He had come to the city in 1949 and walked the streets working as a door-to-door salesman selling imported monkeys as pets. Drawn to theology, however, Jones started (but never finished) a divinity degree.

As the mayor's appointee, Jones was not prone to keeping a low profile and often showed up in local media—particularly about his challenge of local restaurants, hotels, amusement parks and hospitals that still refused service to blacks. In 1961, he and his wife, Marceline, were reportedly the first white couple in Indiana to ever adopt an African American child. Jones made headlines again for purposefully seeking medical treatment in a segregated ward at the Marion County General Hospital (later Wishard Memorial Hospital)—and even called reporters to tell them about it.

As Jones's profile grew, Mayor Boswell and his appointing commission began to learn more about the young pastor. Originally, they viewed him as an outgoing, energetic young man interested in racial integration. The more they learned about his truly interracial church, the Peoples Temple (and its loud faith healing services that alleged to have raised people from the dead and cured cancer), and about Jones's seemingly growing paranoia that Klan interests were trying to destroy him, they were unimpressed. Jones eventually left the commission in 1962, the same year local radio station WIBC pulled his weekly sermons from the air after listener complaints.

Born in tiny Crete, Indiana, near Richmond, Jones never finished his studies at either Indiana University in Bloomington or the Christian Theological Seminary in Indianapolis. Despite that, the Christian Church (Disciples of Christ) readily ordained Jones for ministry—a decision it would later regret.

Jones and his family briefly moved to Brazil—and visited his last home in Guyana—in 1962–63 after he read a magazine article indicating that Brazil may be the safest place on earth in the event of a nuclear war. Settling back in San Francisco, California, Jones's charismatic preaching style and rock-solid commitment to integration played well in the more liberal Bay area of California.

Soon his California version of the Peoples Temple was a growing success. Of the more than four thousand members who regularly attended his church, about one hundred of them were ex-patriot Indianapolis residents who had given up their Hoosier homes and moved to California to join the growing flock. His followers had begun to call him "Prophet." As the *Indianapolis Star* reported in 1972:

> *The handsome, smooth-talking 41-year-old preacher who recites his gospel attired in turtleneck sweaters and dark glasses, claims to also have cured cancer, made the blind see, and the crippled walk. Last fall, when he returned to Indianapolis briefly, several hundred people showed up at the former Peoples Temple to watch the Rev. Mr. Jones "cure" a woman of cancer.*[26]

Despite his growing following, there were detractors, and one of them, Georgia A. Johnson, an Indianapolis mom, gained national attention after the *San Francisco Examiner* published an extensive investigative report on Jones. In it, Johnson alleged Jones had "programmed" her seventeen- and eighteen-year-old daughters to leave Indianapolis and forced one of them (who is white) to marry a black man selected for her by Jones and turn over all their money to Jones and the Peoples Temple.

Back in Indianapolis, local and San Francisco media were uncovering a similar trend: Peoples Temple members who had signed over their homes and other property to Jones and the church. In exchange, they had moved to dormitory-style living quarters in San Francisco or at the church's growing location in Ukiah, California.

The growing scrutiny of Jones and the Peoples Temple furthered his end-times style of preaching that predicted that the end of the world was coming soon and helped convince hundreds of church members to pick up and follow Jones to remote Guyana in Central America. While in Guyana, Jones and his followers attempted to build a perfect Christian community built on socialist principles—known as "Jonestown"—but troubles grew quickly, as did Jones's paranoia, power grabs and drug addiction.

In Indianapolis, news of the Peoples Temple faded, but in northern California, where dozens of followers had grown weary of Jones (and his demands for their money and their relocation to Guyana), more inquiries came. U.S. Congressman Leo Ryan (1925–1978) was finally convinced to lead a fact-finding mission to Jones's Guyana compound in November 1978. A Congressional friend of Ryan's, then U.S. Congressman Dan Quayle, reportedly turned down an invitation to join the trip to Guyana. Among those who did accompany Ryan were former members of the Peoples Temple who wanted to retrieve loved ones who remained under Jones's control.

A surreal visit ensued—captured in books, films and countless documentaries—during which Ryan and his group eventually started to depart with a handful of followers who had had enough of the "sanctuary" of the rugged, tropical Guyana.

Ryan and his entourage, however, never made it out of Guyana. Across the world, headlines carried the news (and eventually video) of the brutal November 17, 1978 assault on Ryan and his party by gun-toting soldiers of the Peoples Temple. In all, nine people lay dead, with nine others injured.

The dead included Ryan, an *NBC News* reporter and cameraman and at least one Temple defector.

Back at the Jonestown compound, the unthinkable was occurring. Jones had successfully persuaded 909 of his followers to drink cyanide-laced fruit punch in the largest mass suicide seen in human history. Three other Jones followers were later found with their throats slit in a grisly murder-suicide at Georgetown, Guyana. Investigators eventually determined that thirty-seven of the people who died at Jonestown were originally Indianapolis residents—almost all of them African American.

A frightening audiotape of the mass suicide emerged months later, and on it Jones is heard leading a sickening scene by encouraging mothers and fathers to give the deadly drink to their children first and then to quietly go on to their own deaths. Jones was found dead of a gunshot wound to the head near the front of the Jonestown worship pavilion.

Former Indianapolis mayor Boswell told reporters that the stories coming from Guyana did not match the Jim Jones he had known. "It seems there'd been a tremendous personality change, the symptoms of which never appeared here," Boswell said.[27]

More than four hundred of the Jonestown suicide victims were buried in Oakland, California, where a monument and annual memorial service is held in their memory. In Indianapolis, few traces remain of Jones's time there. His Peoples Temple location at 945 North Delaware Street is now a vacant lot. His other Indianapolis location, a wood-frame church at 1502 North New Jersey Street, remains and is still in use as a church. The Indianapolis-based Christian Church (Disciples of Christ) also dramatically changed its ordination process for approving new pastors following the Jones debacle.

Elvis and Michael Invade Indy

Two of the biggest names in the history of music, Elvis Presley (1935–1977) and Indiana-born Michael Jackson (1958–2009), both left their marks on Indianapolis—and for very different reasons.

Infamous Celebrities

Elvis's Last Show

The original King of rock-and-roll, Elvis Presley can trace the end of his career to Indianapolis and to his last concert ever on June 26, 1977, at Market Square Arena. Elvis appeared in Indianapolis as early as 1955 in a concert at the Lyric Theatre at Illinois and Ohio Streets downtown. But it was his last show—coming just fifty-one days before his shocking and unexpected death on August 16, 1977—that cemented his connection to Hoosier fans forever.

The Indianapolis concert was the fifty-sixth and last concert that Elvis had scheduled in 1977. Author Susan Doll wrote in 2009 that "[t]he grueling tour schedule and the month-long Las Vegas engagements took their toll on Elvis…[touring] had once been a lifeline to a drowning singing career, was now an exhausting chore; what once had been a challenge to Elvis was now routine."[28]

Presley arrived in Indianapolis from Cincinnati that Sunday "exhausted" and not feeling well. He was whisked to his hotel—the Stouffer Hotel in the 2800 block of North Meridian Street—where he rested until his evening show. "Elvis was so fatigued that the 'Memphis Mafia' were concerned about his welfare," Doll wrote.[29]

Backstage before his MSA show, representatives from RCA presented Elvis with a plaque commemorating the two billionth Presley record pressed by the Indianapolis company. The show went on as expected before a sold-out crowd of eighteen thousand, although not all of the reviews were favorable.[30] "Elvis gave one of his best performances in recent months," Doll reported. "Unfortunately, no one knew it would be the last."[31]

The play list was vintage Presley—"Jailhouse Rock," "O Sole Mio/It's Now or Never," "Teddy Bear/Don't Be Cruel," "Release Me," "I Can't Stop Loving You," "Bridge Over Troubled Water," "Johnny B. Goode," "Hound Dog" and "I Can't Help Falling in Love With You."

Rita Rose, covering the Elvis concert for the *Indianapolis Star*, noted that

> [t]*he big question was, of course, had he lost weight? His last concert here, nearly two years ago, found Elvis overweight, sick and prone to give a lethargic performance. As the lights in the Arena were turned down after intermission, you could feel a silent plea rippling through the audience: "Please, Elvis, don't be fat." And then he appeared, in a gold and white*

jumpsuit and white boots, bounding onstage with energy that was a relief to everyone. At 42, Elvis is still carrying around some excess baggage on his mid-section, but it didn't stop him from giving a performance in true Presley style.[32]

Indianapolis News music critic Zach Dunkin was a little tougher on both Elvis and his show, asking, "Elvis Presley led another crowd of screamers into bananaland last night during his concert in Market Square Arena and the question is why?…Why does Presley still continue to tour? He obviously doesn't need the money. He apparently doesn't care about the way his concerts are packaged either."[33] Dunkin added, "Compared to today's increasingly competitive and sophisticated concert formats for the top-dollar performer, Presley's has become downright tacky and outdated. Last night's lighting was only adequate and the sound was poor compared with some of today's top national tours."[34]

Dunkin wrote a companion story for his review, commenting on the concert and saying that it "had all the flavor of a carnival sideshow," with annoying opening acts and seemingly endless pitches for fans to buy Elvis belt buckles, necklaces, binoculars and pictures in the arena lobby.[35]

Regardless of what the critics wrote, the loyal following at Market Square that evening loved Elvis and cheered wildly when he closed the show by mentioning that the Indianapolis show was the last one of his current tour but that he'd be glad to come back again.

However, there would be no comeback. On August 18, less than two months later, headlines around the world carried the news that Elvis was dead. Questions would be raised forever about the cause of death (and whether illicit drug use contributed to it), but medical examiners in Tennessee have stood by their original declaration that Presley died of heart failure.

Ironically, it was the RCA plant in Indianapolis that worked nonstop for days after Elvis's death to reproduce dozens of his most-loved albums and singles as demand for the King's music soared with news of his death.[36]

Market Square Arena was imploded on July 8, 2001, as the Indiana Pacers moved to their new facility: Conseco Fieldhouse. A special marker inside MSA that commemorated Elvis's last show was saved and was eventually placed back on the former site of the arena.

Michael Jackson Back Home Again

In 2003, Michael Jackson made two separate appearances in Indianapolis to give a deposition in a civil lawsuit that traced back to Gary, Indiana, and the incredible beginning for Michael and four of his brothers: the Jackson Five.

It wasn't a stop that Jackson wanted to make, but it was one that he could no longer avoid. Two men from early in the Jacksons' rise—Gordon Keith and Elvy Woodard—were suing the Jacksons for a variety of copyright issues. Keith, who had founded Steeltown Records in 1967 in Gary, said that he was the first to sign the Jackson Five and wanted a piece of the action (Motown Records had mostly profited from the group). Woodard's suit was based on a claim that he had written two songs that Michael, Jackie, Tito, Jermaine and Marlon had used without his permission.[37]

When Michael finally did testify at the Canterbury Hotel in downtown Indianapolis, it was his second attempt. On his first visit, a week earlier, Jackson suddenly fell ill (reported as an "anxiety attack") and was rushed to Methodist Hospital for observation.

"He has, on some occasions in the past, not eaten when he should," Jackson family spokesman Brian Oxman told Indianapolis reporters. "He can become very concerned and nervous at depositions. He doesn't like lawsuits, and it makes him ill to have to cope with litigation that people seem to heap on him."[38] Once stabilized hours later, Jackson left the hospital, boarded a plane and returned to California.

U.S. District Court judge Philip Simon was unimpressed and ordered Jackson to appear to testify on June 13. Michael's attorneys said that he testified for several hours and declared the lawsuit and its claims as ridiculous—Michael was only nine years old when the alleged breaches occurred. Attorneys for the men suing the Jackson family described Michael as "jovial" during his testimony.

Freed from his legal requirements, Michael created quite a stir as he left his hotel, walked a block to Circle Centre Mall in downtown Indianapolis and visited several stores. A huge throng of fans (many of whom had staked out the hotel to begin with) filled the halls of the mall for their chance to see the "King of Pop."

Seemingly upbeat during his second visit to Indy in a month, it contrasted dramatically with his 1990 stops in the city following the death of his friend Ryan White (1971–1990), the Indiana schoolboy who became famous for fighting for the right to attend school even though he had AIDS. Michael's mood stayed positive the next day as his entourage left Indy for a rare visit to his hometown of Gary, Indiana, where he was presented with a key to the city.

Months later, in December 2003, the Jackson brothers (sans Michael) settled the suit out of court for an undisclosed sum and declared the matter closed. Details of the settlement were not disclosed, although attorneys for the plaintiffs said that "it feels like a victory to us."[39]

Michael's days in the courtroom, despite claims by his lawyers that he hated being in court, would grow larger in number as was arrested in November 2003 on multiple felony criminal charges of child seduction and molestation. It would be the second time that he would face such charges—similar charges in 1993–94 were dropped after Jackson reportedly settled the matter with his accuser for a reported $22 million.

Jackson vehemently denied all of the most recent charges against him, and a surreal trial got underway in January 2005 in Santa Maria, California. After weeks of damaging and embarrassing testimony, the jury acquitted Michael of all charges on June 13, 2005. Almost exactly four years later, on June 29, 2009, Jackson died unexpectedly inside a home in Los Angeles, with a doctor at his side. As with Elvis, many questions remain about why and how the "King of Pop," at age fifty, had died.

THE STATE OF INDIANA V. MIKE TYSON

"You're a nice Christian girl, right?" was what Mike Tyson reportedly said to Desiree Washington just moments before he forcibly raped her inside room 606 of the Canterbury Hotel, one of the toniest sites in Indianapolis.[40]

It was just one of a multitude of disgusting contrasts that would play out in the months following Tyson's Indianapolis arrest—and eventual conviction—for the July 1991 rape of Washington. Washington had come to Indianapolis as "Miss Rhode Island" to compete in the *Miss Black America* beauty pageant. Organizers of the successful Indiana Black Expo believed that they had scored a coup by landing the pageant and worked to invite as many celebrities to attend as possible.

In retrospect, the idea of inviting Tyson to judge a beauty pageant is a bit like asking a fox to watch the hen house, but then (as now), Tyson was a major celebrity and an accomplish boxer. His presence made sense from the standpoint of adding glamour and excitement to the pageant.

In the days leading up to the pageant, Tyson even appeared in an awkwardly taped freestyle dance segment with the pageant contestants. Wearing a "Together with Christ" lapel pin, Tyson spent part of his time in Indy with Reverend Jesse Jackson. Promoters of the pageant videotaped some of the proceedings in Indianapolis and hoped to later package it for broadcast. As it turned out, it was a pageant that no one would want to see.

One of the young contestants enamored of the star status of Tyson, then twenty-five, was Washington, then just eighteen years old and away on her own from her tiny Rhode Island town for one of the first times in her life. It was a whirlwind experience for her—even if it was *just* Indianapolis. Knowing that makes it all the more understandable why Washington accepted Tyson's telephoned invitation to ride around town in his limo and visit his room at the Canterbury. She was so excited that she brought along her camera in the hopes of getting some pictures of herself with Tyson and other celebrities that she could later show to her parents.

Her decision to go with Tyson—however ill-advised second-guessers have said it was—was one that a lot of young people would have taken up. A famous person invites a teenager to "see the town" and become friends; girls and boys would line up for that chance.

Washington, who eventually gave up trying to keep her identity a secret, testified against Tyson in his February 1992 Indianapolis trial that earned international media coverage. As *Time* magazine reported, Washington told jurors about a brutal and demeaning physical and sexual assault that she said ended with Tyson asking her, "Don't you love me now?"[41]

Tyson plunked down a reported $2 million to engage famed defense attorney Vincent J. Fuller (1931–2006), whose previous clients had included would-be presidential assassin John Hinckley Jr. and former Teamsters boss Jimmy Hoffa (1913–1975).

Indianapolis attorney Greg Garrison was appointed special prosecutor for the case by Marion County prosecutor Jeff Modisett because of his extensive litigation experience. Garrison said, "There were one or two members of

Fuller's staff who did not think [that] us country bumpkins could find our asses with both hands."[42]

Ultimately, they underestimated Garrison's charm, his ability to turn a phrase winning him an eventual gig as an on-air legal analyst for *The CBS Evening News with Dan Rather*. Team Tyson also underestimated the victim, Garrison believed: "She's a good kid with a pure heart and a tremendous amount of courage, and she shined like a new penny in front of that jury."[43]

Tyson suffered from having given one account of the night of July 19, 1991, to the Marion County Grand Jury and another account at trial. It created enough doubt to overcome questions about Washington's actions during and after the assault—as well as the "he said/she said" aspect to the case.

The jury found Tyson guilty of one count of rape and two counts of criminal deviant conduct. On March 26, 1992, Marion County judge Patricia J. Gifford sentenced Tyson to six years for each of the three counts—with sentences to serve concurrently. A well-behaved prisoner, Tyson converted to Islam while incarcerated and was released after serving just three years.

During that time, Washington enrolled in Providence College and completed her education but reportedly was greatly changed by her experiences.

Tyson returned to his multimillion-dollar boxing and celebrity lifestyle, often making headlines for outrageous actions and statements. One headline was generated from a particularly startling interview he gave to then CNN reporter Greta Van Susteren. In it, he said of Washington, "I hate her guts. She put me in that state, where I don't know," he said. "I really wish I did now. But now, I really do want to rape her."[44]

Sadly, during the trial, while jurors were sequestered at the historic Indianapolis Athletic Club, a deadly fire ripped through the multi-story building on the night of February 5, 1992. Two Indianapolis firefighters, John Lorenzano and Ellwood Gelenius, were killed fighting the blaze. One of the fifty guests staying at the club was also killed, but none of the Tyson jurors was injured.

CHRIS FARLEY "MILKS" INDY FOR SOME OF HIS LAST LAUGHS

The July 1997 opening of the new Planet Hollywood restaurant at 130 South Illinois Street in downtown Indianapolis was a big deal. It was such a big deal that city officials blocked off streets surrounding the new eatery to accommodate the estimated ten thousand fans who showed up despite a light drizzle of rain. Thousands more watched the festivities live on Indianapolis TV. For Planet Hollywood, it was just the fifty-first (and one of the smallest) new locations in its chain. For Indy, it signaled that the city may have finally arrived.[45]

Several notable celebrities were on hand that night—Bruce Willis, Cindy Crawford and Tom Arnold—along with *Saturday Night Live* alum Chris Farley (1964–1997). No one could have known that night as they watched Farley lumber around, nearly out of control, that this would be one of his very last public appearances ever. Five months later, on December 18, 1997, his brother, Kevin Farley, opened the door to Farley's sixtieth-floor apartment in the John Hancock Tower in downtown Chicago and found his brother's bloated, shirtless body dead on the entryway floor.

It was a sad and ugly end for a comic who had won the hearts of a generation of fans but apparently, as others before, had done so at some cost to himself.

In Indianapolis, the Planet Hollywood opening had added star power because Farley was present, but anyone who watched had to be disturbed. At one point, in between live performances by Willis's band The Accelerators, Farley was on stage with Hoosier-born Indy car and NASCAR racer Tony Stewart accepting a pint of milk—symbolic of the tradition for winners of the Indianapolis 500. But in Farley's typical manic, over-the-top style, he pretended to drink but actually spilled the milk all over his already profusely sweating self. It was an embarrassing moment—imagine Farley spending the evening's events with sticky, drying milk all over his hair and clothing.

Farley's Indianapolis appearance troubled his brother Kevin and friend, Jillian Seely, who had flown to Indy on a private jet with him for the event. Friend and actor Tom Arnold also took note of that night, saying, "The worst I ever saw him was at the Planet Hollywood opening in Indianapolis that July [1997]. It was the bad Chris. I mean, he was just so fucked up. He had his shirt up over his head and people were taking pictures."[46]

Farley's behavior was described by Kevin and Jillian as uncontrollable. "Jillian and I were trying to get him out of the bar, but he didn't want to leave," Kevin Farley said. "At one point, I couldn't control him. Either he's going to take a swing at me and we can get in a fight here in front of the cameras, or I can go home."[47]

Kevin and Jillian decided to leave—without Chris—telling the pilot of Farley's private jet sitting at Indianapolis International Airport to return to Chicago. Jillian described the events this way:

> *We were really quiet on the plane. We were both so sad Chris had started drinking again. The next day I got a phone call around noon. I thought it would be Chris, calling from Indianapolis, confused and wondering why he'd been left behind and maybe having learned a bit of a lesson. But he was like, "Hey, what's going on? I'm back in Chicago. Want to go to lunch?" The plane went right back* [to Indianapolis] *for him and picked him up. No consequences for his actions at all. But his behavior at the party made the* [National] *Enquirer and the entertainment TV shows.*[48]

Farley attended one more Planet Hollywood opening, this one in Houston, Texas, in late October. Local media there noted that "it was 48 degrees and windy and wet, and still Chris Farley was sweating buckets" and that "when Farley reached the stage, they had a rodeo cowboy lasso the hefty comic and hogtie him like a Sunday roast."[49]

Farley's public appearances seemed designed to recreate the bumbling but lovable characters he brought to the small screen on *SNL* and to the big screen in three films (*Tommy Boy*, *Black Sheep* and *Beverly Hills Ninja*).

The roles Farley played—including his famous "motivational speaker" Matt Foley and a larger-than-average Chippendales dancer—weren't ones he always enjoyed. Farley told *Playboy* magazine in an interview published following his death that

> *I used to think that you could get to a level of success where the laws of the universe didn't apply. But they do. It's still life on life's terms, not on movie-star terms. I still have to work at relationships. I still have to work on my weight and some of my other demons. Once I thought that if I just*

had enough in the bank, if I had enough fame, that it would be alright. But I'm a human being like everyone else. I'm not exempt.[50]

When the news broke that Farley was dead, stories referred to him in embarrassing terms, such as blubbery, sweaty, tightly wound, obese, jelly-bellied and flabby, as well as known for characters with "a jiggling gut spilling over his waistband."[51]

A private funeral service for Farley was held at the Queen of Peace Catholic Church in his hometown of Madison, Wisconsin. Fellow *Saturday Night Live* stars Dan Aykroyd, Chris Rock and Adam Sandler attended, along with the show's creator Lorne Michaels, Farley's frequent film costar David Spade and fellow comedians John Goodman, George Wendt and Arnold. Family members asked fans to stay away—a request honored by all but a handful of local high school kids who worshiped Chris Farley and his memorable characters.

A separate service at St. Monica's Catholic Church in Los Angeles drew more of his friends. There, Father Michael Rocha said, "Do I have an explanation [for his death]? I don't. Other than this very jovial, outgoing man had things in his life that were demons, demons that were almost uncontrollable for him."[52]

Back in Chicago, the Cook County medical examiner ruled that Farley had died of an accidental overdose of morphine and cocaine. The coroner said that a contributing factor to his death was a narrowing of the arteries in his heart brought on by his weight, which stood at 296 pounds at the time of his death. Traces of alcohol, marijuana and a prescription antidepressant were also found in toxicology exams.[53]

Reporters quizzed Farley's grieving father, Thomas J. Farley Sr., at his Madison, Wisconsin home. Chris's father, weighing more than six hundred pounds himself, told the reporters, "I'm just getting over [his death]. I know he's in God's hands now."[54]

Chris's father created the Chris Farley Foundation following the comic's unexpected death to help educate young people about the dangers of drug and alcohol abuse. Thomas Farley died in 1999 and is buried near his son. In 2005, the Hollywood Walk of Fame installed its 2,289th star outside a Los Angeles comedy club for Farley.[55] The Indianapolis Planet Hollywood came and went quickly, finally closing in October 1999 under reports of sagging sales and new competition from the nearby Hard Rock Café.[56]

Part II
Infamous Criminals

JOHN DILLINGER ON HIS HOME TURF

Famed 1930s bank robber John Dillinger (1903–1934) is credited with pulling a lot of robberies in his short and violent lifetime, but most of them took place outside of his hometown of Indianapolis.

Dillinger was born on June 23, 1903, in a house at 2053 Cooper Avenue in Indianapolis—a structure plowed under to make way for Interstate 70—in a working-class neighborhood near Twenty-first Street and Hillside Avenue on the city's east side. He attended Indianapolis Public Schools 38 and 55 but never attended school beyond the age of sixteen.

In 1920, the Dillinger family moved from Indianapolis to Mooresville, Indiana, where he was later arrested for the attempted robbery of a grocery store. The local judge threw the book at him, sending Dillinger to the Indiana State Prison from 1924 to 1933, a rather long sentence for an "attempted" robbery. Despite that, Dillinger was productive during his time in prison, learning from some of the nation's best criminals how to be a big-time criminal.

Paroled on May 22, 1933, within months Dillinger was implicated in a series of store and bank robberies across Indiana, Michigan and Ohio. Some of those robberies included the Haag Drug Store at 5648 East Washington Street in the Irvington neighborhood of Indianapolis on June 29, 1933. Witnesses to the robbery said that Dillinger wore a white cap and dark glasses during the heist.

Dillinger (and presumably now his "gang") made even bigger headlines with the September 6, 1933 robbery of the Massachusetts Avenue State Bank at 815 Massachusetts Avenue (just northeast of College Avenue). The bold, noonday crime netted Dillinger a reported $24,800.[57]

Witnesses inside the bank told police that two armed men entered the bank, while a third waited outside in a getaway car. Outside on the busy downtown street, other witnesses described a second car holding five other heavily armed men, including one man holding a machine gun. Both cars outside the bank were reported to have Ohio license plates and were later determined to be stolen vehicles.

"Six patrons of the bank were compelled to stand quietly while one of the bandits, who was masked, vaulted the partition of the cashier's cage," the *Indianapolis News* reported. He then ordered the bank manager and teller to give him the cash. In their haste, the robbers overlooked $5,000 in additional cash in a second drawer.[58] It seemed that following the Indy heists of 1933, Dillinger and his gang moved on to other locales, perhaps to take the heat off his remaining family in Indianapolis and Mooresville.

Neighbors to Dillinger's brother's home at 409 North LaSalle Street on the city's east side were quick to call police in April 1934 when they believed that John was visiting. Police responded with a fury, since Dillinger had just escaped from the Lake County Jail at Crown Point, Indiana, on March 3, 1934. Indianapolis police, however, were always a step behind the slick Dillinger. Federal and state police also kept a close watch on Dillinger's aging father in Mooresville as the multiple-state hunt to catch Dillinger intensified.

Dillinger's actions—some he committed and others that were just attributed to him—were told in terrific detail in Indianapolis newspapers until July 22, 1934, when headlines carried the news of Dillinger's death in a shootout with federal agents outside a Chicago movie house.

A macabre and bizarre series of events followed as Dillinger's body was placed on display in Chicago, and then in Indianapolis, for a parade of onlookers to see. *Time* magazine described the odd events surrounding Dillinger's death:

> *In a wicker basket aboard a hearse, the body of John Dillinger rode home last week from Chicago's morgue to Mooresville, Ind. There it was dressed in a light suit, fitted into a $165 coffin, and taken to his sister's bungalow outside*

Grave site of John Dillinger, Crown Hill Cemetery. *Photo by Steve Polston.*

Indianapolis. During the night, 2,500 mourners filed past all that was left of the year's worst killer. Next afternoon a quartet opened the burial service by singing "God Will Take Care of Him." Father John Dillinger sat motionless in shirtsleeves…The quartet closed the service with "We Say Good Night Down Here and Good Morning Up There." Down thumped the lid of the coffin. The cortege set out for Indianapolis' Crown Hill Cemetery where President Benjamin Harrison and three Vice Presidents rest in peace. As rain began to fall, breaking the long heat wave, the body of John Dillinger was lowered into a grave beside that of his mother. Rev. Fillmore intoned, "Yea, though I walk through the valley of the shadow of death…" The dirt was shoveled in.[59]

THE ART OF THE DEAL GOES DEADLY WRONG

Houses along North Meridian Street in Indianapolis are often referred to as "mansions," and it's an apt reference. During the early part of the twentieth century, North Meridian Street above Thirty-eighth Street was home to some of the city's wealthiest and most famous and powerful citizens.

Now considered a historic district, protecting the noteworthy homes from improper development, famous residents have included Pulitzer Prize–winning author Booth Tarkington (1869–1946); there is also the Indiana Governor's Residence at Forty-sixth and Meridian.

The home at 4285 North Meridian Street served as an office to real estate developer Stanley A. Selig, fifty-two, who operated his business from a parlor there. Just before 11:00 a.m. on March 11, 1970, Selig's office would become a gruesome crime scene as an angry real estate investor barged into the home and shot Selig dead.

Police arrived just moments after five fatal shots pierced Selig through the face and stomach and arrested William Clarence Jones—identified as a forty-nine-year-old resident of Anchorage, Alaska—who had traveled to Indianapolis to "have it out" with Selig.

Jones told police that he had been battling Selig for return of his $29,000 investment in land in Brazil, South America. Jones had sought the help of the federal government in trying to ensnarl Selig for what he believed were bogus mail-order real estate deals. Selig's secretary, Barbara K. Salzmann, told police that when Jones first arrived Selig was not present but rather arrived shortly afterward.

"The two men went into Selig's office and the matter of a large sum invested in Brazilian land was discussed," the *Indianapolis Star* reported from Salzmann's account. "Miss Salzmann also said she heard some mention of postal authorities, and the discussion became loud."[60]

Salzmann said that Selig emerged from his office and asked her to call the police because Jones was causing a disturbance. Within ninety seconds of her first call to police, Salzmann called back, saying that she had heard gunshots from inside Selig's office.

As police arrived, Jones remained inside the home office, and they removed two loaded handguns from the man. In the years before the shooting, police learned, Jones had purchased—sight unseen—16,439 acres of land in Brazil. The land was in the central highlands area of Brazil in the state of Goiás. When Jones visited the land for the first time—he realized that he had been had. The land was barren, rocky and inaccessible except on foot. It was not suitable for any residential or commercial development.

After returning to the United States, Jones also spoke to officials in the U.S. Attorney's Office to try and make them force Selig to refund the money.

Selig and his brother, real estate fixtures in Indianapolis since the 1940s, announced in 1966 that they had purchased 3 million acres of land in Goiás, what they called "a fertile plateau" at 2,500 feet above sea level.[61]

A year later, Selig was called before a Brazilian government panel that ordered him to pay $67,000 in taxes on the land. In 1968, an Arizona man filed a complaint with the Brazilian government saying that he had been sold 1,200 acres of land that he could not precisely locate in the tropical territory.

Selig's business dealings had gotten him into trouble before. Just two years earlier, federal marshals seized about $13,000 in goods from the Esse Surplus Company in Indianapolis, owned by Selig. Federal authorities accused Selig and his associates of illegally removing tools and other valuables as the company was in bankruptcy receivership.[62]

The *Indianapolis Star* uncovered that when inquiries were sent to Selig about the land in Brazil, he would produce a brochure that included color photographs of modern buildings in Brasilia (about four hundred miles away from the land actually owned by Selig) under a caption that read, "An invitation to meet at the foot of the rainbow to divide the pot of gold."[63]

Jones had reason to be angry. An $8-an-hour steamfitter and welder originally from Jonesboro, Arkansas, he had sold his home there at a profit of $5,000 in order to make a down payment on the land in Brazil. He also signed a contract with Selig and began making $740-a-month payments for the land. He had made six of those payments before he saw the land and believed that he had been swindled.

Police learned that Jones had visited Selig once before about his concerns but had been assured "not to worry" about the land deal. He came armed with guns for his second visit, the day Selig was killed.[64]

TONY KIRITSIS: MAD AS HELL AND NOT GOING TO TAKE IT ANYMORE

Time magazine, in its coverage of the Tony Kiritsis case that became a national story, noted that Kiritsis was a lot like "a peculiar, but harmless figure on big-city streets, the lone man walking down a sidewalk, railing loudly at some injustice inflicted by a distant, impersonal tormentor. The angry man who acts out his rage usually appears only in films…but sometimes he appears in real life."[65]

Peculiar, loud, railing and raging—all of these accurately described forty-four-year-old Kiritsis, the son of Greek immigrants and a bartender from the working-class neighborhoods of the west side of Indianapolis. Despite his simple beginnings, Kiritsis wanted to make it big in business. By February 8, 1977, Kiritsis had turned from a hopeful, driven businessman to a dangerous potential killer.

On that day, Kiritsis walked into the Market Street offices of Meridian Mortgage Company, pulled a pistol on the president of the company, Richard O. Hall, forty-one, and then set about wiring Hall's head to a sawed-off shotgun with the safety removed. The wire around Hall's neck was attached to the trigger, meaning if Hall attempted to break free, his head would be blown off.

From there, Kiritsis called the Indianapolis Police Department, just a block east of the mortgage office, and informed them that he had taken Hall hostage and had wired him to "a dead-man's line." He warned police: no one had better act like a hero.

After that, in a short-sleeved shirt with no jacket, Kiritsis proceeded to march Hall east down the snowy sidewalks of Market Street to Pennsylvania Street, then south on Penn to Washington Street and then west. Astonished workers and shoppers on the sidewalk that day scrambled for cover, with IPD officers trying to keep a handle on the situation while also keeping their distance.

Kiritsis continually shouted profanity and threats to anyone who got close as he continued west along Washington Street, briefly startling police as he and Hall slipped on the snow and ice and fell to the ground at the intersection of Illinois Street. The gun didn't go off, and Kiritsis recovered his balance and continued to march Hall westward while refusing to talk to the cops and threatening to kill Hall.

Just past the Indiana Statehouse, Kiritsis ordered an IPD officer to abandon his police cruiser and handcuffs and, with that, summarily ordered Hall behind the wheel of the cruiser, and they fled west. For the next sixty-three hours, Hall would be held captive in the bathroom of the modest apartment that Kiritsis kept at Crestwood Village Apartments.

Dumbfounded but determined to get Hall released unharmed, IPD and the FBI set up camp at the clubhouse at the apartment complex and opened a long and difficult dialogue with the irrational Kiritsis. Kiritsis also spoke frequently live on the air with Fred Heckman, a newsman from Indianapolis's top AM radio station, WIBC. The media seemingly played a big role in all of Kiritsis's plans, as he demanded that Hall's company should not only relieve him of the now defaulted mortgage but also read a statement of apology on live television.

The anger stemmed from the pending foreclosure action that Hall and Meridian Mortgage were pursuing against him for a $130,000 mortgage that Kiritsis held on a seventeen-acre parcel of land. The land, some of which would eventually become part of today's Lafayette Square Mall area on the west side, was ripe for commercial development, but Kiritsis blamed Hall and his father for driving away potential commercial partners for the land because he believed they wanted the land for themselves.

The latest mortgage loan payment was due on March 1, and Kiritsis had failed in earlier attempts to get Hall to extend the payment deadline. "These people have betrayed me," he told Heckman in a live interview. "I went down there for vengeance, and by God, I'll have vengeance."[66]

During the standoff at Kiritsis's apartment, he emerged with Hall (his bleeding neck now visible from the strain of the wire) in order to air a twenty-three-minute diatribe about the wrongs that he believed had been committed against him. Most Indianapolis television stations carried the statement live. At first, Kiritsis ordered Hall to read his statement but then suddenly yanked the paper away from the hostage, complaining that he was not reading it in a way people would understand.

Getting people to understand Tony Kiritsis would be a challenge, it seems. Prone to rambling and interrupting himself with side thoughts not related to his original point, Kiritsis declared that "I am completely sober, my friends. I had six drinks in 1976, and I haven't had any this year."[67]

Strangely trying to find the lighter side of the moment, Kiritsis shoved the gun deeper into Hall's neck and declared, "I told this man that before this thing was over, he would think I was a God-damned witch. I read him all these things, all these charges that are on that paper that I typed up a couple of months ago, as I tried to recall back over four years."[68]

Interrupting himself, he glanced down at the gun and said, "I hope this damn thing doesn't go off, I'm having too much God-damned fun," and again shoved the rifle into Hall's neck.[69] "I said, ladies and gentlemen, that these people were lucky they were dealing with me. I haven't got a God-damned nerve in my body, and you're God-damned lucky. A nervous nelly would have blown his God-damned brains out a long time ago."[70]

In a surreal attempt at sympathy, he confessed that "I can tell you, by God, that I was in trouble, I was in a hell of a lot of trouble. You saw one of these God-damned things off [motioning to the shotgun] and kidnap somebody, I'm gonna tell you something, there ain't much left for you down the road."[71]

As tears began to stream down his face, the gun-toting Kiritsis said, "I am pleased that a lot of nice people who have called me the last couple of days, and told me they were behind me, and I want to thank them, and I want to thank my brothers."[72]

Convinced that he was succeeding in getting an apology, having his mortgage debt erased and being given $5 million and immunity, Kiritsis eventually released Hall from the mechanism, but not before firing the gun in the air once to prove that it was loaded.

Following his subsequent acquittal in court by reason of insanity, he told reporters outside the courtroom, "We all live in the greatest country on earth, but this is the type of thing that undermines the liberties that my father and my mother came here from Greece for, and probably all of your ancestors. And I'm not trying to be corny. I may be a flag-waver, but I wave it a hell of a lot better than John Wayne does, I'll tell you that."[73]

Ordered confined to an Indiana state mental hospital, Kiritsis remained lodged there from 1977 to 1987, when he was released and agreed to continue to see a psychiatrist regularly. In 1990, he filed suit against 101 separate individuals whom he held responsible for his arrest in 1977—cases that were later dismissed. Kiritsis died in June 2005 at the age of seventy-two. Hall has never commented publicly on his ordeal.

THE SPEEDWAY BOMBER

As the Labor Day weekend got underway on Friday night, September 1, 1978, Speedway police and fire officials were caught off-guard as three separate bombing incidents that caused damage, but no injuries, rocked the tiny village enveloped by Indianapolis. Best known worldwide for its annual hosting of the Indianapolis 500 each May, Speedway was normally a quiet town the other eleven months of the year.

The first blast came at 9:50 p.m. from a trash container on a sidewalk outside the Hi-Fi Buys store at the Speedway Shopping Center along

Main entry, Indianapolis Motor Speedway. *Photo by Steve Polston.*

Crawfordsville Road. Ten minutes later, another blast ripped the dumpster behind the famed Speedway Motel along West Sixteenth Street near the main entrance to the Indianapolis Motor Speedway. Finally, at 10:45 p.m., another explosion went off along a residential street just west of the speedway in the 1600 block of Whitcomb Avenue.

The shopping center bomb blew out windows at the stereo store and an adjacent shop. At the motel, the dumpster was moved several feet from its original spot several feet, and trash was strewn about the parking lot, but no motel windows were damaged.

Police were baffled about what was going on but thankful that no injuries had occurred. "We don't have too many explosions here, let alone three in one night," Speedway Police Department corporal Gary Donaldson told the *Indianapolis Star*.[74] No information was received from police warning of the blasts, and no one claimed responsibility for them. They were as random as could be.

Speedway police quickly called on bomb squad experts from both the Indianapolis Police Department and a U.S. military unit from Fort Benjamin Harrison to assist. Eventually, thirty bags of debris were collected, with investigators declaring the bombs to be of a "cheap" and "low grade" design.[75]

Speedway police chief Robert L. Copeland told reporters that anyone with a basic knowledge of chemistry could have made the bombs but that they were made so that the person setting them in place could escape before they blew.[76]

Two more blasts would come on Saturday—both in vacant lots that caused little damage—although one was set off just half a mile from the Speedway Police Department headquarters. The federal Bureau of Alcohol, Tobacco and Firearms confirmed that the bombs were similar to the three earlier ones: a metal soda pop can packed with gunpowder and a rudimentary timing device.

A sixth blast came on Sunday evening just before 10:00 p.m., in a parking lot outside the Speedway Lanes bowling alley, just east of the Motor Speedway. The small blast caused minor damage to the building and nearby parked cars.

"We still don't have a suspect or a motive," said W. Cummins Beaty of the ATF. "Just no idea of who it is."[77]

At 9:50 p.m. on the same day when Beaty made his remarks, a seventh bomb went off, this time one planted underneath the patrol car of an off-duty Speedway police officer. The officer, on sick leave, was not present to see his patrol unit nearly destroyed, along with heavy damage to adjacent vehicles.

Surely a trend was developing: the bombings all took place at about the same time and were contained only to the Speedway community. By now, about one hundred ATF and FBI agents had been assigned to report to Indianapolis to assist in the probe.

"Now we know we've got a real nut," Speedway chief Copeland said. "There's no rhyme or reason to this thing. Police headquarters could be next."[78]

As in the previous cases, remnants of a six-volt battery were found, along with gunpowder and a timing device. But the worst was yet to come, as just one day later an eighth blast occurred in the parking lot of Speedway High School, this time just after 8:10 p.m., injuring three people, one of them critically.

Police later determined that Carl D. DeLong and his wife, Sandy, both thirty-nine, were leaving a junior varsity football game at the school when they spotted a small gym bag on the ground near their car. As Mr. DeLong picked it up, a mighty explosion was heard, hurtling him through the air and dropping Mrs. DeLong to the ground. Car windows all throughout the parking lot were shattered.[79]

As many as a dozen other parents were either going to or already waiting in their cars for their sons to emerge from the school locker room at the conclusion of the game. Amazingly, no other injuries were recorded, and the DeLongs' son, Steve, escaped injury as he was still inside the school when the blast occurred.

As paramedics rushed the injured couple to the hospital and police cordoned off the school, the latest in a series of ultimately false bomb threats came in—this time claiming that a bomb was planted inside the Speedway Cinema at the Speedway Shopping Center. Police quickly evacuated the theater during a movie showing, but no bomb was found.

As no motive has ever been determined for the bombings, it was unclear why they stopped, but the bomb that seriously injured the DeLongs was the last to rock the small town.

It was not the last of the tragedy to touch Speedway in 1978. On November 18, four young workers at the town's Burger Chef restaurant along Crawfordsville Road were abducted and later found executed in a Johnson County farm field. No arrests were ever made in that case.

An arrest was forthcoming in the bombing cases, however, as twenty-seven-year-old Brett Kimberlin was picked up by federal authorities on September 20, 1978, for attempting to obtain illegal federal identification documents and uniforms from an Indianapolis firm. While held on that charge, police were able to search his 1970 Chevrolet Impala and found wiring and some blue and white "Mark Time" appliance timers—sold at only one store in the Indianapolis area.

With that, detectives took a lineup of pictures to the store that sold the "Mark Time" devices, and the workers all identified Kimberlin as the man who had purchased them. In addition, a previously undisclosed eyewitness from the first bombing identified Kimberlin as the man he saw placing a parcel in a trash can just before it exploded.

The tangled tale of Kimberlin would forever get more complex. Police searched a southern Indiana property owned by his family and located there a large underground tank holding more than one thousand pounds of marijuana. They also located two cases of Tovex 200 dynamite and traced them to Kimberlin in a 1975 transaction.[80]

ATF investigators positively identified remnants of the blue and white "Mark Time" devices as matching those taken from Kimberlin's car. With evidence mounting, federal prosecutors moved forward in presenting their evidence to a federal grand jury, which subsequently indicted Kimberlin.

It would take three tries, but federal prosecutors finally succeeded in convicting Kimberlin on twenty-two counts as the "Speedway bomber" in October 1981. A previous trial, in the fall of 1980, ended with a hung jury on the bombing counts, but a conviction on charges related to his attempts to obtain fraudulent Department of Defense security credentials allowed officials to keep him incarcerated as they prepared for a new trial.

During his trials, attorneys for Kimberlin attempted to portray him as a victim of a vast government conspiracy. They noted that he was a "successful businessman"—he owned a small natural foods and earth shoes store in Broad Ripple, which police said was just a front for dealing narcotics.[81]

Kimberlin proved to be a difficult prisoner, filing civil suits against many of the witnesses against him and threatening the rest with similar actions. After his conviction, police released yellow legal pads they had confiscated from him that they said detailed his plans to kill key witnesses and prosecutors and rob and intimidate others.

Even more troubling, as Kimberlin awaited trial, one of his suspected coconspirators, his younger brother Scott E. Kimberlin, twenty, was shot and killed on October 20, 1980, with his own gun in a mysterious case in Dayton, Ohio.

Another murder had suggested ties to the case. The mother of Kimberlin's close friend, Sandra Barton, was mysteriously executed on July 29, 1978, just before the Speedway bombings began. Julia Scyphers, sixty-five, had disapproved of Kimberlin's alleged sexual interest in her preteen granddaughter (Barton's daughter) and made her views known.

Mrs. Scyphers suffered a single gunshot wound to the back of her head inside the garage of her home at 1651 Cunningham Avenue in Speedway. She had gone to the garage to show a man who knocked on her door some of the items that she had for sale. Her husband, Fred Scyphers, sixty-eight, eventually identified one of Kimberlin's friends as the man who came to the home that day, but Mr. Scyphers died of cancer on March 14, 1979, and no one was ever charged in his wife's murder.

Although no motive for the bombings was ever disclosed, some investigators believed that the bombings may have been a diversionary tactic to move police off their probe of Mrs. Scyphers's execution-style murder.[82]

Another death could also be tied to this case: Carl DeLong. DeLong lost his lower right leg and two fingers in the bombing, and both he and his wife had painful shrapnel imbedded in their bodies for years. Mr. DeLong was hospitalized for six weeks and underwent nine separate surgeries to repair his remaining left leg, which had also been severely injured. Numerous surgical attempts were made to help relieve Mr. DeLong of pain from bomb fragment injuries that also damaged his inner ear, stomach and arms. After suffering years of pain and surgeries, Mr. DeLong was found dead of an apparent suicide in the garage of his home in February 1983. His family later won a large civil settlement against the now penniless Kimberlin.

Kimberlin was eventually sentenced to fifty-one years in prison for the Speedway bombings but was released in 1994 after having served thirteen years. He was returned to prison, however, in 1997 after making no effort to pay the civil penalty won by the DeLong family. He remained jailed until he was finally released in 2001.[83]

The "Yogurt Connection"

One-time Hoosier Abraham Lincoln (1809–1865) is often quoted as saying, "You can fool some of the people all of the time, and all of the people some of the time, but you cannot fool all of the people all of the time."

A more apt description of Linda Leary and her sons couldn't be said. On one side of their life, Leary and her sons, Paul and Richard Heilbrunn, were community leaders in Indianapolis. Linda had served a term as president of the local chapter of the League of Women Voters and another term as head of the local chapter of the National Council of Jewish Women.

Paul Heilbrunn was a successful businessman who wrote a column for a local business journal. The family jointly owned a YoGo yogurt shop franchise, a popular Indianapolis eatery. Their connection to the kosher yogurt shops would later earn their criminal enterprises the name "Yogurt Connection."

In fact, it wasn't until a fifty-three-count federal indictment was handed down against Mrs. Leary and her sons in November 1987 that most people in Indianapolis knew that there was another side to their lives. The indictment charged that from 1975 to 1987, Leary and her sons "led a gang of up to 100 members that ran an estimated 250,000 pounds of

Colombian, Jamaican and Thai hemp worth $50 million to $100 million into the Midwest."[84]

"No one thought people who played tennis at the club and did good work with the League of Women Voters could also be criminals," former U.S. attorney Deborah Daniels said about the trio.[85] In fact, Leary and her sons had defenders for a long time before specific details about their "other life" began to emerge. After all, Linda Leary was involved in local politics and helped raise funds for the new downtown Indianapolis Zoo.

But under the surface, there were problems that had existed for many years but may have been papered over because of Leary's strong connections to local political leaders. Twice divorced, Linda was raising her two teenage sons alone, who quickly became known as the go-to guys for anyone who wanted to buy pot at North Central High School in the 1970s. Leary's neighbors would later say that she was lax with her sons on what they did in an effort to be "the cool mom."[86]

Richard graduated from North Central in 1975 and started up a garage-based business purportedly to sell Dr. Bonner's Natural Castille Soap. The demand for the soap must have been tremendous, because soon Heilbrunn and Friends (as they called their enterprise) leased a warehouse and Paul quit high school to help run the business. The "business" was really about supplying marijuana to colleges and universities throughout the Midwest and to street dealers in at least eleven midwestern cities.

Over time, Paul began to run the business enterprises, which often traded off the family's good name and position in society. One unidentified source told *People* magazine in 1989 that they readily took $70,000 in cash from Paul for a short-term lease of a remote Indiana barn—with the agreement that they ask no questions.[87]

Trouble surfaced publicly for the first time in September 1975 when Richard was shot and wounded by an alleged drug dealer who owed the brothers money. A second man in Richard's company that day, John Jenkins, was shot and killed. No charges were ever brought (as the suspect eventually killed himself before he could be apprehended), but a rift opened between Richard and Paul. For her part, Linda told family and friends that the shooting was the result of an argument over a business deal for "health food."[88]

A key factor to the success of the Yogurt Connection, it seems, is that Richard and Paul were not heavy drug *users*. They enjoyed all of the benefits that the money selling drugs created (and so, eventually, did Linda), but they were not known to use drugs themselves. The pot business was going strong for them—federal investigators estimated the value of their enterprise at more than $50 million at its height—the Yogurt Connection allegedly at one time storing as much as 250,000 pounds of marijuana in two locations in Indiana and Michigan.

One of their lieutenants, however, *was* a drug user and soon found himself fired by the brothers. Under arrest on other charges in 1983, the former trusted member of the Yogurt Connection began to spill what he knew about Linda, Richard and Paul.

As the intensity of the federal investigation grew and came closer and closer to Linda and her sons, the family began spending more and more time at their vacation home in the Bahamas. Eventually, one of those trips in 1985 never ended, the family fleeing to Austria to avoid prosecution back in Indianapolis. It wasn't as if they knew that they weren't a target—Richard had testified before a federal grand jury early in 1985 and understood that he and his family were targets of the probe.

By the end of 1987, Linda and her sons were under federal indictment back home. Linda faced twelve counts, including conspiracy to distribute marijuana, money laundering and interstate transportation in aid of racketeering. Paul faced twenty-six counts, including conspiracy to import and distribute marijuana and running a continuing criminal enterprise. Richard was charged on nine felony counts. In all, thirty-four people were indicted in the case.

The family, however, was not feeling cooperative. Attorneys for them indicated that they were doubtful of their chances to get a fair trial in the United States, and they set about using all of their resources to avoid arrest and extradition (until those assets were frozen). The trio wasn't arrested by Austrian police, in fact, until May 1988, seven months after they were indicted, and were later released.

Frustrated, American prosecutors at Indianapolis noted that "at this point it's completely in the hands of the Austrian government. Obviously, I would feel better if I were in control, but that's just the way it is," said Deputy U.S. Attorney John Thar.[89]

Finally, in December 1989—two years after they were indicted—Linda, Richard and Paul were extradited to the United States and, following a preliminary hearing, were housed at the Marion County Jail in Indianapolis.

Overwhelmed by the case against them—and now in her sixties—Linda Leary cut a deal with prosecutors and pleaded guilty to helping her sons run the marijuana operation. In August 1990, she was sentenced to nine years in prison for drug dealing and a concurrent five-year sentence for racketeering. The racketeering charge stemmed from Mrs. Leary's control of a trust account in the Cayman Islands used to launder marijuana profits, prosecutors said. She ended up serving just two years of her sentence, earning a release from federal custody in June 1992.[90]

In April 1991, Richard and Paul Heilbrunn took their medicine and entered guilty pleas admitting that they had engaged in drug dealing, money laundering and racketeering. Richard's forty-five-year prison sentence was reduced to thirteen years under the plea agreement, while Paul's sentence was reduced to twenty-eight years. Richard ended up serving less than four years, earning his release in September 1994. Paul was released in June 1992, just two months after his mother's sentence had ended.[91]

THE KMART BOMBING LEADS TO HEALING, FORGIVENESS

A routine trip to a Castleton-area Kmart store almost turned deadly for Erin Bower and her family in April 1989; the randomness of the incident placed fear in the heart of any parent who has ever went shopping with a curious child.

A pump-style tube of Crest toothpaste misplaced away from all the other toothpaste—positioned between boxes of garbage bags in the home care section—was too much for a little girl to resist.

"I touched everything I saw," Erin recalled more than decade later. "I picked up the Crest pump bottle and immediately saw red and blue wires and knew something was wrong. Picking it up detonated it. Setting it back down made it explode."[92] The tube of toothpaste was a bomb.

Inside the tube of toothpaste was gunpowder and a layer of BBs intended to increase the shrapnel effect, investigators from the Bureau of Alcohol, Tobacco and Firearms later determined. They never figured out how long the tube had sat there before Erin's tiny hand touched it, but they did eventually learn who placed it there.

"I don't remember that much. I just remember not being able to see," Erin said.[93] Witnesses told of a horrible scene—a loud explosion and a small puff of smoke rising from one of the Kmart aisles, followed by loud screams of pain from Erin and panicked calls for help from her parents.

"The husband had his child in his arms, running around, the mother was screaming," an unidentified Kmart employee told television reporters. "[The girl's] hand, I'm not sure how much, but several parts were actually blown off, and there was a lot of blood on her stomach, and it burned her clothes all through [her mid-section]. We ran and we got ice, 'cause, you know, to put her limbs in, and water, and, you know, everybody tried to help out."[94]

Fortunately, an off-duty Carmel firefighter and emergency medical technician and a medical student from the Indiana University School of Medicine were both in the store at the time. John Moriarty, the firefighter, was shopping for a G.I. Joe doll for his son. "I heard the explosion and took off in that direction when I heard the screams," Moriarty recalled. "I heard the mother yell, 'Oh my God,' and two screams from a child. Then I heard the father say, 'Someone please help my baby' over and over again."[95]

Moriarty reported that debris and smoke still filled the air—smoke that smelled like sulfur to him—as he ran to assist. He saw Erin's father, Kevin Bower, looking dazed and holding the limp body of his daughter in his arms, her winter coat still smoldering from the smoke.

"I got to the father and advised him I was an off-duty firefighter and EMT and I could help him," Moriarty told reporters. "I asked the med student who he was and he said he was a third-year med student specializing in trauma. I knew we could work together."[96]

The med student, Louis Profeta, took charge and tried to stabilize the girl as police and ambulances raced to the store near the junction of East Eighty-second Street and Allisonville Road. Moriarty ordered bystanders to run and get the store's first-aid kit, while Profeta asked another to get pillowcases from a nearby shelf to help stop the bleeding.

The girl, only semiconscious from her injuries, was covered in blood all over her face. Moriarty used some of the pillowcases to grab remnants of the girl's hand in the hopes that they could be saved. Kmart workers also brought garbage bags and ice to hold the severed hand and lower arm.

Moriarty said that it wasn't until after they had grabbed pillowcases and trash bags that he paused to think—there could be more bombs planted elsewhere on the store's shelves.

Erin was air-lifted via LifeLine helicopter to Methodist Hospital in downtown Indianapolis, where doctors worked feverishly to save the child's life. Chances to save her hand and lower arm were gone—the damage was just too severe, and an amputation below the girl's right elbow was completed. Erin's mother, Maureen, was also slightly injured. Her father and her younger sister, Megan, were not harmed.

Charles Peterson, the local agent in charge of the Indianapolis ATF office, said that the toothpaste tube bomb "was a little more sophisticated than the average pipe bomb. Some knowledge and thought went into it, and it appears construction of the device was intended to hurt someone."[97] Peterson said that the bomb, although wrapped in a pump-style tube of Crest toothpaste, was "an electrically fired metal pipe bomb."[98]

Police immediately evacuated the Kmart store and all adjacent stores. In the hours that followed, no other bombs were found, and Kmart immediately offered up a $5,000 reward for information about who had committed this horrible crime.

Erin was hospitalized for three weeks recovering from her injuries and eventually was fitted for a prosthetic arm and hand. Despite ten separate surgeries, however, doctors eventually were unable to restore vision in her right eye, also terribly injured in the blast. It was replaced by a glass eye.

"I knew Erin would never be the same again," Maureen said. "No matter what, without a hand and without vision…at that point, we didn't know if she would see at all. And I kept thinking to myself that I never would have had children if I'd known how bad this would hurt. That's how I felt."[99] As Erin's life slowly returned to normal, she quickly went back to school at St. Puis X Catholic School and learned to adjust with her new prosthetic arm.

ATF investigators continued their work, stymied in part by the reported suicide of a person they considered a top suspect. Just two days after the Kmart bomb exploded, Hamilton County sheriff's deputies responded to a call and found the lifeless body of David L. Swinford, nineteen, in his car on a rural county road. Swinford had died of a self-inflicted gunshot wound to the head.

It took another year, but in April 1990, ATF officials announced that they were closing the case and named Swinford as the sole person responsible for the bomb. The forensic evidence linking Swinford to the bomb was solid, they said. As the bomb was made, a sharp tool was used to cut a hole in the top of the toothpaste tube in order to make a switch. That tool left marks—ones that exactly matched those made by a knife found in Swinford's car on the day he died.[100]

Further lab tests revealed that a screwdriver found in the trunk of young Swinford's car was used to tighten the screw on the arming device of the bomb. BBs and wiring consistent with those used in the bombs were also found.

Some of Swinford's family members were initially skeptical, and all were understandably heartbroken. Someone from his family, however, had contacted authorities the day after the bombing, wondering aloud if David could have been involved.[101]

"I wouldn't think that David would want to hurt anyone," said his mother, Gracie Rogers Whitesell. "If he did do it, I could see why he committed suicide. That little girl looks exactly like his 4-year-old sister, Paula."[102]

ATF agent Peterson said that Swinford had struggled to get along with his parents and had recently been asked to move out of their Noblesville home, despite gaining a recent promotion to manager of a local Burger King.

"He and his parents were discussing the bombing the night of April 17, 1989, and they said something like, 'What a terrible person must have done this,'" Peterson said. "In response, [David] said something like, 'I'm sure who ever did it didn't mean to hurt a little girl.'"[103]

For Erin, more than a decade after the bombing, it was clear that she held no grudge. "He wanted it to make a loud noise, maybe scare someone. I guess the bomb turned out to be stronger than he thought," Erin told *Indianapolis Woman* magazine.[104]

"I'm sure this boy had no idea what consequences were going to take place," Maureen said.[105]

"I think it was more of a practical joke and it actually hurt someone, it hurt me and once he found that out, I think he didn't know what to do," Erin added. "I don't think he could live with that thought[106]...I feel horrible for [David's] family, they lost more than what my family lost," she said. "I have forgiven him."[107]

In 2001, Swinford's mother wrote a letter to Erin Bower expressing her sorrow and revealing how much the bombing had weighed on her heart and mind in the intervening years. The Bower family sued no one—not Kmart and not the Swinford family.

Instead, Erin Bower went on with her life and in 2009 completed a master's degree in physical therapy so that she can help others injured as she was. Part of her work brings her into contact with the med student who helped her that night in the Kmart store, Louis Profeta, who is now an emergency room doctor at St. Vincent Hospital, where Erin also works.

"I just want to show everyone that I am doing great," Erin told Anne Ryder of WTHR-TV for her "Hope to Tell" series. "Bad things happen to good people, and if you work through it, you'll be fine."[108]

INDIANAPOLIS VICE

Prostitution and vice of some sort exist in almost every small, medium and large American city, and Indianapolis is no different. Often described as similar to a tide rushing in on a beach, eras of prostitution seem to ebb and flow depending on the determination and the imagination of local officials in arresting it.

Indianapolis has never possessed a well-defined red-light district, per se, in part because local officials have been, at times, quite vigilant in running off undesirable elements, especially prostitution operations. From 1896 to 1917, however, "commercialized vice was permitted and sometimes favored by the city administration," reported the *Journal of Social Hygiene* in 1919. "Prostitution practically became legalized. Prostitutes registered their names and locations at police headquarters, and they were protected and operated practically under the authority of the officers of the law, yet in direct violation of the law."[109]

As early as 1859, the city had enacted ordinances regarding public morality, decency and order, one of its earliest ordinances in 1863 declaring that

> [e]*very prostitute found wandering about said city, or within one mile from the corporate limits thereof, or found in any public act of prostitution within said city limits, shall, on conviction of such offense before the Mayor of Indianapolis, be fined therefore in any sum, not less than five, nor more than fifty dollars.*[110]

The ordinance seemed to be a good idea, as early volunteers of the Indianapolis Fire Department brigades took it upon themselves to become "moral guardians" of their neighborhoods and "burst into houses of prostitution, hosing down the occupants and ruining the interiors," notes the *Encyclopedia of Indianapolis*.[111]

Just a year later, public records show that Molly Green of Indianapolis appealed her conviction under the ordinance. The charge against Green noted "on the 27th day of June, 1863" that she "did unlawfully keep a house of ill-fame and prostitution" and was fined fifty dollars.[112] She lost her appeal.

By the turn of the century, the issue of prostitution in Indianapolis and elsewhere had seemingly turned into a discussion of public health issues rather than criminal code violations. Repeated references to efforts to stem the tide of venereal diseases spread via prostitution are referred to in meetings of Indiana State Medical Association. The ISMA, however, did not avoid discussion of the legal issues involved and engaged in lively debate over whether prostitution should be legalized, regulated or "segregated" into specific areas of the city.[113]

The ISMA heard from advocates who said that

> *there must be education of the people against prostitution and towards a pure family relation…the development of pure and simple home and family life, early marriage, more children in families, and the restriction of divorce are to be the highest, greatest factors in the combat with venereal diseases.*[114]

By 1911, child labor and welfare advocates had stepped up their efforts to combat the abuse of child labor in Indianapolis and elsewhere and focused on exposure of children to prostitution and the city's red-light district as a powerful weapon in their effort. The Indiana Child Labor Commission, in fact, heard provocative reports from Dr. Edward N. Clopper of the National Child Labor Commission about troubling occurrences in the Circle City. First up, focus on the city's well-developed bicycle messenger service and its activities after 9:00 p.m. each night—activities "almost exclusively in connection with the evil features of city life," Dr. Clopper told the commission members. He added the general public was "ignorant [of] the evil influences surrounding the night messenger service."[115]

Western Union messenger boys, Monument Circle, circa 1908. *Library of Congress LC-USZ62-105658.*

Dr. Clopper's investigators had interviewed several messenger boys and found them eager to deliver messages to and from female prostitutes and their customers, as well as procure opium and other drugs for downtown hotel patrons. Dr. Clopper declared that

> [t]*he uniform or cap of the messenger boy is a badge of secrecy and enables him to get liquor at illegal hours, or to procure opium or other drugs…hence these boys are thrown into associations of the lowest kind, night after night, and come to regard these evil conditions as a normal phase of life. Usually, the brightest boys on the night force become the favorites of the prostitutes; the women take a fancy to particular boys because of their personal attractiveness and show them many favors, so that the most promising boys in this work are the ones most liable to suffer complete moral degradation.*[116]

Dr. Clopper shocked commission members by retelling the story of an eighteen-year-old Indianapolis boy working as a messenger who was "afflicted with a horrible venereal disease" and had been working with prostitutes—perhaps even as one himself—for five years beginning at the age of thirteen. "There is a girl who wanted to keep me," the boy told the child labor investigators. "She said she would furnish money to support us both. There are lots of women who keep boys and the fellows just work for appearances."[117]

The Indiana General Assembly did pass a broadly stated "White Slave Law" during the 1911 session, but it mostly dealt with women brought into the state for the purposes of prostitution. It did not specifically address local laws, such as the ones Indianapolis had enacted that included special penalties for police officers who lingered too long in the company of vice operators.

Controversial Hoosier Eugene V. Debs (1855–1926)—the five-time Socialist Party nominee for president—wrote once in 1915 that "working men are forced into war as working women are forced into prostitution"[118] and meant what he said. Often swimming against the tide, Debs made headlines earlier in 1913 when he went to Indianapolis and retrieved a "scarlet woman" who had been "arrested on the street by police for immorality" and took her to the Terre Haute home he shared with his wife in an attempt to "redeem her."[119]

Debs challenged his fellow Christians—Socialist or not—to consider something:

> *What would Christ do? The police have told her she must keep off the streets or go to the red light district. Do the police mean to get recruits for the red light district? If that is the police policy toward women, then to be consistent, the police should compel immoral men who stand on the streets, to stay in the red light district. The men who hunt girls are more dangerous to society than women. It is time for this pitiless cruelty to stop. Why not war on the immoral people in high life, instead of persecuting this penniless girl.*[120]

In 1917, the American Social Hygiene Association singled out several U.S. cities for their efforts to combat prostitution and venereal disease, efforts assisted by the federal War Department. In Indianapolis, they noted that the state's new Injunction and Abatement Law had been used effectively in its first years of existence by bringing twenty-four lawsuits against the owners of properties used for prostitution and other vice. As a result, "more than 60 houses of prostitution have been vacated."[121]

Local officials singled out the work of the Church Federation of Indianapolis, whose members took it upon themselves to personally investigate suspected houses of prostitution and send the property owners and the county prosecutor notice of what they had uncovered. They also focused their efforts on "lewd" theatrical performances in the popular downtown burlesque houses along West Washington Street.

Prostitution in the city's African American neighborhoods had been a particular police focus at times, while white areas were often ignored. Dr. G. Henri Bogart, a medical doctor writing on why women become prostitutes, said that he had specifically studied "Negro joints" along Indiana Avenue in Indianapolis in 1916 and declared that some girls started as prostitutes after falling victim to incest or molestation. "These colored prostitutes come from every section of the South," Dr. Bogart wrote. "Indianapolis is a Mecca for the 'bad nigger' of the southern states…[and] the connection [between] drink and drugs to prostitution is most clearly seen. These habits rarely induct the young woman into a life of vice, the habit comes later."[122]

Depending on what party or mayor controlled city hall, it seems that the ebb and flow of prostitution in the city's downtown and adjacent neighborhoods continued. In the early 1970s, Indianapolis appeared to be a lot like many other big cities in America. The *New York Times* reported that the breakthrough X-rated movie *Deep Throat* had played for weeks in the city to large audiences and that "[i]n Indianapolis, the police now count 19 massage parlors within the city, and a half dozen more within its environs, and 'not more than one of them is a bona fide massage establishment,'" Indianapolis Vice Squad lieutenant Reed L. Moistner told the paper.[123]

Moistner said that police had successfully forced open prostitution off Indianapolis streets, but "now they're into this," and "it's even harder to arrest here."[124]

Investigative reporters from the *Indianapolis Star* turned their attentions to the issue of vice and its connection to the city's police department in the 1970s as well. A handful of indictments followed that revealed that the city's number one madam, Mary Martin, had enjoyed a comfortable relationship with city police for years.[125]

Martin operated dozens of homes on the city's near north side along formerly tony streets, such as Delaware, Alabama, Pennsylvania, New Jersey, Park, Central and College Avenues—transformed into whorehouses as white flight continued to move the city's white families farther and farther from Center Township. The *Star*'s investigation showed that a large number of bad cops readily accepted cash or sexual favors to look the other way. Then Indianapolis mayor Richard G. Lugar (now a U.S. senator) survived the brewing scandal by sweeping house at the IPD. The *Star*'s reporters on the series—William E. Anderson, Dick Cady and Harley E. Bierce—captured a coveted Pulitzer Prize for special localized reporting in 1975.

A year later, Indianapolis prostitution made national news again, this time in *Jet* magazine, a publication geared to African American readers. *Jet* trumpeted that twenty-eight-year-old Charles Harris, aka Charlene Harris, of Indianapolis was the first man in Indiana to be sentenced to prison for being a prostitute. "Indiana's prostitution law changed in 1975 to include men—which changes the name of hookers to 'persons of leisure,'" *Jet* reported.[126]

Male prostitution in Indianapolis hit the headlines again in 1990 when William Dayton, a computer scientist at the Naval Avionics Center in Indianapolis, dropped dead quite unexpectedly in his hotel room. Dayton left behind records indicating that he was at the top of a thirty-nine-state male hooker operation employing one hundred prostitutes—complete with meticulous records on more than three hundred male clients. It was a sensational story from the start, with police and prosecutors teasing the public with news that

> the clients and prostitutes included Indianapolis bankers, a Cincinnati priest and a Marion County police officer…the clients and prostitutes were drawn from 39 states, Canada, South Korea and Guam…Dayton is believed to have matched at least 100 prostitutes with 300 patrons through a sophisticated electronic network that sought clients through advertisements in homosexual magazines.[127]

Marion County prosecutor Steve Goldsmith (later mayor) told reporters that "we have dozens and dozens of prostitutes, and we have hundreds of customers and patrons. We have a ring involving tens of thousands of dollars and a substantial health hazard, we believe, for the city of Indianapolis."[128]

Interest in the case soon dwindled, however, with cops and prosecutors holding tight to the list of clients; only a handful of prosecutions ever materialized.

Part III
Infamous Disasters

Train Disasters Have Left Their Mark

It seems that as long as there have been trains, there have been accidents, and Indianapolis has witnessed some of the deadliest crashes in the nation's history.

The Monon Crash

The January 1890 crash of a Monon passenger train just north of the city in what is today Carmel, Indiana, is one of the earliest known. In that crash, six of the eighty-five passengers on board were killed—another twenty-five seriously injured.

The passenger train was operated by the Indianapolis Air Line division of the Monon Railroad and left Chicago at 11:55 p.m. on January 26; it was scheduled to arrive at Union Station in downtown Indianapolis the following morning at 8:30 a.m. The train, however, "met disaster a half mile beyond Carmel" just as it crossed a long trestle over Wilkinson's Creek in Hamilton County. "The truck of the engine jumped the track before the bridge was reached," reported the *Indianapolis News* in a dramatic account. "The engine and the baggage car cleared the trestle safely, but the remaining cars went over it into the creek and took fire" just before 8:00 a.m.[129]

The *News'* headline declared "Six Passengers Killed Outright or Roasted in Burning Car—Injured Twenty-Five" in a scene described as one of "frightful disorder."[130] For many, the scene was reminiscent of an earlier train bridge collapse into the White River near the Broad Ripple area of Indianapolis in January 1884 that left several dead.[131]

Reporters indicated that local residents helped scoop the dead bodies from the creek, although they had lain on the creek bank for several hours before being retrieved and taken to local mortuaries. Engineers on the train reported that "when the ladies' day coach reached the center of the bridge, it fell through with a crash to the depths below. The wreck thus created took fire from the stove and that car was entirely consumed. It was in this coach that all of the casualties occurred." A sleeper car also fell from the bridge but did not catch fire.[132]

Purdue University Football Players Perish

Amid claims that "never in the history of the city was so much interest manifested in a football game," Indiana and Purdue university football teams prepared for their annual battle for 1903, in a game to be played at Washington Park on the eastside of Indianapolis.

"Next Saturday will be football day in Indianapolis," the *Indianapolis Star* declared. "Indications are that the city will celebrate the day with all the enthusiasm of a university town and that the pigskin-chasing athletes will be warmly received."[133]

The game was to feature a new invention, a "patent score board" that would allow spectators to not only see the score but also the down number, yards to go and which team had possession of the ball. Ultimately, it was a game never played.[134]

Excitement was at a peak in both Bloomington and West Lafayette as well, and in the latter, the Big Four Railroad Company had chartered two trains to carry about 1,500 fans from West Lafayette to Indianapolis for the big game. The first train, however, met disaster as it collided with a parked coal train sitting on the tracks on October 31, 1903. The engineers of both trains were unaware that another train was on the same line. The rail line where the crash occurred no longer exists but ran virtually parallel to today's Interstate 65 near where Twenty-first Street and Dr. Martin Luther King Jr. Boulevard intersect.

Of the 963 people aboard the "special," 17 were killed, 13 of them members of the Purdue University football team; 48 people suffered injuries. Survivors of the horrible crash ran northwest along the tracks to warn the next Purdue special, and it avoided hitting the back of the crashed first train.

An investigation showed that the ten-car coal train was actually backing up northward into the path of the southbound Purdue special. The engineer of the Purdue train attempted to brake, but an incline and curve in the track made that impossible. He estimated that his travel speed was thirty miles per hour when he struck the coal train.

The "uproariously boisterous and almost deliriously happy" passengers on the train were "changed to tears and sorrow in the twinkling of an eye," wrote the *Indianapolis Star*.[135]

The Associated Press reported that "the trains came together with a great crash, which wrecked three of the passenger coaches; in addition to the engine…the first coach on the special train [which carried the football team] was reduced to splinters."[136] A second coach slid down an embankment next to the tracks, and a third coach slipped off the tracks to the other side.

"A wild effort was made on the part of the imprisoned passengers to escape from the wrecked car…and immediately following the wreck, the students and others turned their attention to the work of rescuing the injured."[137]

Purdue University president Winthrop E. Stone (1862–1921), who survived the crash, offered thanks to those who had come to the aid of the injured students, "particularly to the people of Indianapolis, who have spontaneously proffered every possible aid to the afflicted students and to their families, our heartfelt thanks due…This catastrophe was appalling, but it has revealed the noblest qualities of humanity."[138]

Head-on Collision of Two Interurban Cars

Another deadly crash occurred just northeast of the city in what is today the Geist-Fortville area on February 2, 1924, just as Indianapolis newspapers carried the news of the death of former president Woodrow Wilson (1856–1924). This crash, just west of the settlement of Alfont, involved two Indiana Union Traction Company interurban trains that collided head-on, killing sixteen and injuring forty others.

Initial reports from the scene were grim, the Associated Press dispatching that

> [n]*ine badly charred bodies have been removed from the two cars that were destroyed by fire and seven other bodies are believed to be in the wreckage… The cars were of wooden construction and all that remained of them was a mass of smoking embers and red hot brake rods and tracks. Each train consisted of a meter car and trailer. The motor cars were telescoped and most of the dead and injured were in these cars. The motormen on both trains escaped with slight injuries as they jumped before the collision.*[139]

The westbound train had left Anderson and the eastbound train from Fort Harrison in Lawrence, with the crash occurring at about 5:15 p.m. on a Saturday evening. The conductors of both trains gave conflicting accounts about their instructions on how to proceed, with the coroner trying to determine whether to hold members of the interurban crews on manslaughter charges. The president of the train company acknowledged that "automatic block signals" on the line were not in operation and that written orders for the conductors of each train were lost in the resulting inferno. He defended his employees as "experienced, trustworthy and well-qualified men."[140]

One survivor, Minnie Waymire, a nurse from Indianapolis, gave a frightening account, noting that "the victims prayed, moaned, cried and screamed for help as the flames swept toward them. The moans of those conscious but held helpless while the flames slowly licked towards them were terrible…Only after the fire had done its terrible work did the moans of the unfortunate victims stop. It was the most terrifying scene I could imagine."[141]

Reporters spared readers no grisly details, the *Anderson Daily Bulletin* reporting that

> *a gruesome spectacle greeted those who were admitted to the morgue to view the bodies. Five of the blackened remains were headless and only the charred trunk of the bodies remained. The terrible condition of the bodies that had been literally cooked in the human funeral pyre made identification difficult…only the blackened backbone remains of one of the victims.*[142]

Five days later, the macabre details continued to flow, the *Anderson Daily Bulletin* carrying a front-page story noting that the "charred head of a baby" had been found in the train wreckage.[143]

The Sahara Grotto Club Crash

Another train tragedy that shook the people of Indianapolis occurred on Friday night, October 14, 1927, when an interurban train plowed into a trailer carrying Halloween partygoers from the city's Sahara Grotto Club. Seventeen passengers were killed and two others injured.

The crash occurred along Emerson Avenue on the city's east side just after the group had set out from its gathering point at Washington and Emerson Streets, near the Grotto clubhouse. The trailer was struck by an interurban train operated by the Indiana Union Traction Company, the same company whose trains had collided three years earlier in a deadly crash near Fortville.

"The party had gathered in light-hearted congeniality…less than a half hour before more than a score of persons were crushed in the compact of the interurban crash. Eagerly husbands, wives and daughters mounted their queer equipage and set out on a novel trip to the stolid old barn which awaited them," reported the *Indianapolis Star.*[144]

Survivors said that the group had just begun singing "Show Me the Way to Go Home" when the crash occurred. The singing quickly stopped, the *Indianapolis News* reported, as the interurban train

> *smashed into the trailer, without striking the truck proper, with the traction car scattering bodies to both sides of the track for a distance of 200 feet, some of the mangled forms found several yards from the track. When the traction car finally came to a grinding stop a quarter of a mile from the crossing, six bodies were found on the pilot of the traction car.*[145]

The Sahara Grotto, identified as a branch of the Mystic Order of Veiled Prophets of the Enchanted Realm, was a popular social club among men involved in local Masonic lodges. The Sahara Grotto party was organized in honor of the club's "Drill Team."[146]

The day after the crash, manslaughter charges were filed against the motorman and conductor of the interurban car and against the driver of the truck that pulled the trailer full of party revelers. The truck driver told police that he did not hear or see the interurban train approaching the crossing, which had no automatic signals in place. Other witnesses, however, claimed that they heard the whistle on the interurban train "blowing frantically."

The *Indianapolis News* reported that "a long row of automobiles parked at the curb of Emerson Avenue and Washington Street all night long aroused curiosity" until it was determined that the cars belonged to the doomed Sahara Grotto party members. "Some of them never will come back...and even Saturday morning some of the automobiles had not been claimed, and the police were seeking to return them to the families of the dead owners."[147]

"LITTLE HEROES OF THE STREET"

The April 18, 1905 front page of the *Indianapolis News* carried an etching depicting newspaper boys hovered over by the Angel of Death as the city's residents tried to grasp the tragedy of four young boys trampled to death in stampede.

Residents of Indianapolis were gasped into silent shock as the news spread that a free theater ticket giveaway had so excited a band of newsboys that a panicked stampede had taken place, crushing four of them, ages eleven to fifteen, to death. Another thirty-one boys were injured—the youngest just eight years old. Immediately, questions were raised about how this could have happened—what could have prompted such an incredible and sad event?

The day's events started normally enough. More than six hundred boys from across the city were summoned to attend a special meeting at the Masonic Lodge located at the corner of Washington Street and Capitol Avenue. There they could retrieve free theater tickets—a rare treat for young children in 1905—to attend a show at the Unique Theatre in downtown Indianapolis. The ticket giveaway was sponsored by a local philanthropist to aid the newsboys, many of whom came from some of the city's poorest families.

At 7:20 p.m., the tickets were distributed "to the glad 'newsies'" inside a second-floor hall at the Masonic Lodge. "The tickets were distributed and the boys were told to walk to the street and line up, preparatory to marching to the theatre on East Washington Street," the *Indianapolis Star* report explained.[148]

Indianapolis newsboys await that day's edition, circa 1908. *Library of Congress LC-DIG-nclc-03221.*

Indianapolis newsboys with police officer, circa 1908. *Library of Congress LC-USZ62-105662.*

Once the boys had their tickets in hand, they were "transformed into a panic-stricken mob when, in leaving the building to march to the theatre, there began a pushing and shoving which resulted in a wild rush to the bottom of the stairs, where four boys met death beneath the heels of their comrades," the *Indianapolis Star* reported.[149] The narrow staircase—apparently the only exit route for the large group of boys with theater tickets in hand—could not handle the rush, and a gruesome scene unfolded.

It is not clear if the boys started pushing and shoving for fear of not getting a seat at the theater or from unconfirmed reports that someone unwisely yelled "Fire!" and the large crowed reacted in panic.

"When the boys started to leave the hall, they pushed and shoved and within a few seconds, many were tumbling down the stone steps leading to the street," the *Star* report continued. "Those following were piled on top of the boys who fell first. Within an incredibly short time, the lads were piled 10 high in the stairway and hallway."[150] A Masonic Lodge meeting was occurring at the same time on the first floor of the building, and those men quickly responded and pulled more than one hundred boys to safety.

"As soon as the police arrived…the injured lads were lined on the sidewalk in front of the hall," the *Star* reported. "The line of suffering lads presented a terrible sight…passing pedestrians lent willing hands and did all they could for the boys."[151]

Panicked parents quickly overran the city's general hospital, where the injured boys were taken for medical treatment. After the site was cleared, reporters indicated that "blood dripped down the steps" and "fragments of clothing and flesh were strewn here and there."[152]

Curiously, most of the uninjured boys went ahead and attended the free show at the nearby Unique Theatre, the showing continually interrupted by panicked parents looking for their boys as word of the disaster spread across the city.

"The management of the theatre, dazed by the terrible catastrophe, scarcely knew what to do, but finally threw open the doors to the boys and told them the show would be given," the *Star* reported. About five hundred boys attended the show, while some of their mates were either still trapped or were being hauled off to the hospital.[153]

The show was ended after the second act, however, as the parade of parents and police coming in and calling out specific boys' names was too much of an interruption to go forward. The actors in the play refused to go on.

"The boys were reluctant to leave, and it was not until the statement was made that the show would simply be stopped, that they finally consented," noted the *Indianapolis Star*.[154]

The *Indianapolis News*, in a poetic moment about the newsies, some of whom among those killed or injured carried the *News*, noted:

> *Their little playmates wounded, dead! These little ones*
> *still heard to call of duty, and did meet*
> *Disaster, choking back their tears. Poor "newsies";*
> *The noble little heroes of the street.*[155]

DEVASTATING FIRES SEARED INTO INDY'S HISTORY

Fires have played a devastating role in the history of Indianapolis, though with advances in fire safety, fire prevention and protection equipment, the loss of life and property has been greatly reduced over the city's history.

The Bowen-Merrill Fire

The deadliest fire in the city's history took place on St. Patrick's Day 1890 as smoldering flames broke out in the basement of the Bowen-Merrill Company, a paper goods company situated just west of the corner of Meridian and Washington in the heart of downtown. Before it was over, thirteen of the eighty-six Indianapolis firefighters called to the scene that March day had died.

Smoke was reportedly first noticed coming up from steel grating in the sidewalk in front of the store, indicating a fire in the basement. The first firefighters on the scene underestimated the severity of the fire and the fact that flames had crawled up inside the building to upper floors. Eventually, the building was fully involved, and the roof and upper floors of the building began to collapse, trapping and killing firefighters.

As the *Indianapolis Journal* reported, "What ought to have been a one-thousand-dollar blaze, at the worst, unattended by loss of life or causalities of any kind, developed yesterday afternoon into a destructive fire, accompanied by a frightful sacrifice of human flesh and blood."[156]

The *Journal* account noted that firefighters remained on the building's roof even after the fire had been burning for almost two hours. Eyewitnesses reported that the roof's flat surface "seemed to sag in the middle, slowly at first, and them more rapidly, and sent its brave human freight down toward the horrible crater. In vain did the poor fellows grasp at the [fire] hose that trailed, like a snake, at their feet, but seemed to elude them when they would have seized it. The arms of some of them waved wildly in the air, cries of despair leaped from their throats and then came the crash."[157]

The National Surgical Institute Fire

Just two years after the horrible loss of life in the Bowen-Merrill fire, another sad tragedy struck as a fire broke out inside the National Surgical Institute during the early morning hours of January 21, 1892. The fire blazed quickly through the wooden structure that housed 316 physically disabled patients on the northeast corner of Georgia and Illinois Streets in downtown Indianapolis. In the end, 19 patients with severe disabilities were killed, and 30 others were injured.

The National Surgical Institute had been founded in Indianapolis in 1858 by physicians committed to the treatment of all surgeries and chronic diseases. It was the first of its kind in the United States, and the institute quickly became known for its ability to assist people with severe physical deformities, particularly "club foot," harelips and hip and spinal deformities. The institute also manufactured and sold surgical and mechanical implements for the treatment of these types of cases and was a growing concern by the time of the fire.

Accounts after the fire indicated that the building had been renovated many times, with new wings and rooms added—all of wood construction. The hallways of the institute were also reportedly very narrow, as were the nine stairwells that provided exits from upper dormitory floors of the four-story building.

Heroic accounts of patients being saved filled the pages of the Indianapolis newspapers:

> *A short time after the fire burst forth from the roof…a* Sentinel *reporter saw a large number of the smaller children taken from their cots in the two rooms on the upper floor by the men who started back over the route by which*

they had come up… [but] *the stairs leading down from the third floor to the second floor are contracted and narrow…the exit from the south and north hall of the second floor opens on a narrow, rickety stairway that trembled warningly as the men found their way onto it and down to the street.*[158]

The *Indianapolis Journal* reported on a group of children evacuated to safety inside a nearby restaurant—one boy, described as a "cripple from Iowa," asked someone to bring snow in from the street to put on the burn blisters on his feet.[159]

By the next morning, freezing temperatures cast what was left of the buildings into an ice sculpture. Firefighters digging through the rubble came across a mother and child both burned to death, "two human trunks glued tightly together in a horrible cooking process they have undergone, grasping one another in death's last embrace."[160]

The fire was the source of tremendous outcry and shame. "Since the buildings had been declared fire hazards more than 10 years earlier, the tragedy created a public outcry and spurred building code and safety reform in the city," reports the *Encyclopedia of Indianapolis*. The institute closed forever in 1898.[161]

The St. Vincent's Hospital Fire

Panic proved deadly after a fire broke out in April 1904 at St. Vincent's Hospital, located at Delaware and South Streets in downtown Indianapolis. Further complicating matters, when the St. Vincent's alarm sounded, dozens of Indianapolis firefighters were already on the scene of a fire at the one-hundred-room Occidental Hotel, also downtown.

The St. Vincent's Hospital, the second infirmary in the city, consisted of private rooms, an operating room and an operating theater used for teaching.[162]

As the fire raged, hospital personnel eventually calmed frightened patients and helped more than one hundred of them escape without injury. One nurse, however, was fatally injured as she jumped from a fourth-floor window to escape the blaze. Others were injured when the rope they had fashioned out of bed sheet failed them as they climbed down from the third floor.

"Many of the patients who had undergone operations became frantic and made violent efforts to escape," the *New York Times* reported. "The attendant physicians were fearful that fatalities may result to those whose wounds from operations had not yet healed."[163]

Within two hours, smoke was cleared from the building, and patients were returned to the rooms not damaged by the fire. The cause of the fire was traced to an electrical problem.[164]

The hospital faced another major event on June 6, 1908, when a gas explosion from the Prest-O-Lite building located next to the infirmary blew out windows in the hospital and injured patients.[165] In 1913, the hospital moved its historic building to Capitol Avenue and Fall Creek Parkway, near where Ivy Tech Community College stands today. It remained there until 1974, when its facility on West Eighty-sixth Street was opened.

Tomlinson Hall Destroyed

On a cold winter's night in 1958, "rocketing flames roared through Tomlinson Hall…one of the city's most famous landmarks," cried the morning editions of the *Indianapolis Star* on January 31, 1958.[166] Despite such emotion, the *Star* report indicated that by the 1950s, Tomlinson Hall "was regarded as an eyesore, and the city wondered what to do about it."[167]

Indianapolis firefighters were able to save the City Market "addition" in the '58 blaze, which remains today. The original entrance to Tomlinson Hall is also intact, but all other remnants of the building were lost. The fire gutted the attic and second story of the imposing building situated on the northeast corner of Market and Delaware Streets. Its massive assembly hall hosted hundreds of important community meetings in the city's history, dating back to when the hall was first opened in 1886. Presidents and vice presidents of the United States have spoken within its walls, Rudolph Valentino (1895–1926) performed there once and the facility temporarily housed victims of the 1913 floods in Indianapolis.

Tomlinson Hall was a "massive brick structure possessed of large hip roof towers at each corner and a triple arched main entrance covered by a balcony supported by heavily carved limestone brackets," explains the *Encyclopedia of Indianapolis*. "The upper floor was a large performing hall, designed to seat 4,200, with a stage capable of accommodating 650 people. The acoustically impressive auditorium possessed oak paneling, grand chandeliers, and comfortable theatre seats."[168]

Nursing Home Fire Claims Twenty Lives

A horrible fire on December 17, 1964, claimed the lives of twenty elderly patients cared for at the Maples Convalescent Center in the tiny Indianapolis-area settlement of Fountaintown. Thirteen other patients suffered burns and other injuries as they struggled out into the snow and temperatures of three degrees above zero in their pajamas.

The convalescent "center" was actually a two-story, sixty-year-old farmhouse converted into a new use, situated along U.S. 52 (Brookville Road), just west of State Road 9. The home's oil furnace, eventually ruled to be the cause of the blaze, was working overtime to keep up in single-digit temperatures. Complicating the fire, renovations of the home over the years had covered over two fireplaces that, firefighters said, eventually acted as deadly ventilators for the fire.

The home was staffed during the overnight hours by three employees—ages fifty-six, sixty-two and seventy-six. One of the attendants smelled smoke at about 3:00 a.m. and notified the other two nurses on duty. They worked feverishly to try to move residents from the fifteen double-occupancy care rooms inside the home and out of danger. Many of the frail and elderly residents resisted, afraid to go out into the cold night. Those who died were all aged between seventy-one and ninety years of age—similar in age to those who escaped but were injured.

One of the nurses, Myrtle Donahue, suffered injuries as she led, dragged or carried eight women and two men to safety. "There was one patient who weighed 240 pounds and I couldn't lift her, so I got her into a wheel chair. There were flames and smoke and she fell out of the chair, so I dragged her out by the wrists," Mrs. Donahue told reporters.[169] "There was another patient too heavy to carry," she added. "I put her on a straight-backed chair and tipped it backward and dragged her out that way."[170]

One of the first volunteer firefighters on the scene said that the home was fully engulfed in flames. "We heard a woman screaming," said Bob Reed. "The chief and I could hardly get in the front door. We had to crawl under the smoke and fire. The chief got a hold of the woman's foot and I dragged her out. She was so badly burned, I can't see how she survived."[171] Reed added, "We heard the other [patients'] screams, but we couldn't get to them. It was a regular inferno."[172]

Indiana state trooper Ronald White was also an early responder and told reporters that "I found five people, all dead, in their beds."[173]

Immediately, questions were raised about the quality of care offered at the Maples, with the workers and neighbors saying that the residents there were happy, but state nursing home records showing that the facility had struggled to meet ever-increasing care standards. Because it had been opened before new rules were enacted in 1958, nonambulatory patients were allowed to be cared for on the second floor (apparently expected to use a metal tube fire escape on the side of the home in the event of an emergency).[174]

"Although authorities said the Maples Convalescent Home had 'poor' health standards, these conditions were not responsible for the tragic pre-dawn blaze," the *Shelbyville News* noted state fire investigators reported.[175]

The Grant Fire

Workers in skyscrapers in downtown Indianapolis stared out their windows in amazement during the early afternoon hours of November 5, 1973, as a massive blaze ripped through a huge portion of the Washington Street corridor, leveling almost an entire city block. Amazingly, no deaths and no serious injuries were recorded.

The four-alarm blaze started in a vacant storefront of the W.T. Grant building on the south side of Washington Street, between Pennsylvania and Meridian. At one point, the inferno threatened the historic Merchants National Bank Tower, which firefighters saved by spraying it with water for hours. As the five-story Grant building burned out of control and began to collapse, flames engulfed the adjacent seventeen-story Thomas Building and eventually leveled it as well.

Amazingly, flames fueled by twenty-mile-per-hour winds jumped the street and ignited buildings on the north side of Washington Street as well. Dramatic scenes played out as flames poured from the top three floors of the seventeen-story Washington Hotel just east of the Meridian-Washington intersection. As the fire grew in intensity, city officials ordered scores of downtown buildings evacuated, and workers were ordered to go home. In the end, fifteen buildings were damaged or destroyed—ironically just a block from the city's deadly Bowen-Merrill fire in 1890.

Investigators eventually traced the source of the fire to construction work going on inside the Grant building.

THE "GREAT PANDEMIC OF 1918" CLAIMED 1,632 INDY LIVES

Considering by today's standards the mortality statistics resulting from the "Great Influenza and Pneumonia Pandemic of 1918" in Indianapolis, it is difficult to conceive the level of human suffering and loss experienced here and around the world.

"Like a runaway train, the epidemic is gaining steam," a Boston newspaper declared in early 1918. "The whole city is stricken," a Gloucester, Massachusetts nurse said. "We were taken quite unawares."[176]

Just as the population centers of the East were caught unaware, seemingly so was Indianapolis. Officially, the first cases of flu were reported in Evansville in far southwestern Indiana on September 20, 1918. By September 25, cases were appearing in Indianapolis. By October 1, the flu had spread nearly statewide throughout Indiana.

Spread of the disease was perhaps made worse by the reaction in some quarters to preventing its spread. Public health officials were seemingly split over the value of both quarantines for people exposed to the virus and the prohibition of large public gatherings (including school, work and church). There was even disagreement about the value of cloth face masks that were distributed en masse by the Red Cross and many other community organizations.

On October 7, 1918, the *Indianapolis Star* carried the news that "Indianapolis schools, churches, theaters and moving picture houses were ordered closed and a ban was placed on all public gatherings yesterday by the city health board. The order is effective this morning and will be in effect for an indefinite period."[177]

The health board's ban, coming as about two hundred flu cases had emerged in the city, ran into the very real problem of how to enforce it. There were many who remained skeptical about the seriousness of the flu or the methods to prevent it. Interestingly, the *Star*'s front-page story about the public health order ran far below ongoing coverage of World War I from across the sea.

A variety of other actions followed, including placing placards in the front yards of families who had members sick with the flu. And there was, of course, the continued rise in deaths as dozens and eventually hundreds of people fell ill and died. Mortuaries across the city were overrun and struggled to provide adequate caskets and burial rites for the departed.

In November, with the flu still raging in Indianapolis and across the nation, the city's board of health announced that it would continue to enforce a face mask order for residents. This came after the board heard from local physicians about the emergence of more than 130 new cases in one day in the city.

The Indianapolis health officials believed that the face mask order would "permit the business and social activities to continue with as little hindrance as possible. The board members were unanimous in declaring for the efficacy of the gauze mask, but the citizens of the city, they say, will be the factor to determine whether its use will have the effect of bringing under control the spread of a serious epidemic."[178]

The board's order read as follows:

> *The wearing of the mask is urged in all public assemblies, such as theaters, churches and other places where there is a danger of contagion by the breath of germ-laden air created by persons with respiratory infections...The wearing of the mask is a scientific precautionary measure which will aid in the suppression of influenza and contagious pneumonia. Therefore, every citizen is requested to cooperate with the board in wearing the mask in public for the protection of himself and fellow citizens.*[179]

Schools were also ordered to remain closed despite continued questions about the board's authority to do so. Rebellious acts continued to be reported—in one, a South Bend, Indiana priest was arrested after he refused to call off Sunday Mass for his parishioners. Local school officials were also among those who were opposed to the strict efforts undertaken.[180]

The same newspapers that carried questions about the actual risk of the flu also carried stories that indicated that of the more than 3,200 deaths statewide in less than two months, more than half of the affected were between the ages of twenty and forty, resulting in more than 3,000 Indiana children being made orphans.[181]

Regardless, the pressure on health board members continued, and just a day before Thanksgiving, newspapers carried the news that the board had reversed itself and lifted the face mask order. Local schools, however, were to remain closed.[182]

Before it was over, more than 150,000 Indiana residents were infected with influenza between September 8, 1918, and March 15, 1919. Statewide, 14,120 Hoosiers died, 1,632 of them in Indianapolis during that period. The Indianapolis mortality rate of 4.6 deaths per 1,000 citizens was double that of the overall statewide rates and higher than the mortality rate for the much larger city of Chicago.[183]

Dorothy Ritter Russo wrote in her *One Hundred Years of Indiana Medicine*: "It is probable that it will never be definitely settled where the severe and fatal form of influenza arouse in the fall of 1918…[but] truly influenza was a killer more to be feared than the German Army, one easily invading the home front, slaying soldiers in cantonment and civilian in his own domicile with equal facility."[184]

Fort Harrison's Deadly History

In the spring of 1945, the United States military began a slow but steady reduction in force as the last battles of World War II were coming to an end.

Victory in Europe Day (VE Day) was observed on May 8, 1945 as Allied forces accepted the unconditional surrender of Nazi Germany. On August 6 and 9, 1945, U.S. forces dropped the world's first atomic bombs on the Japanese cities of Hiroshima and Nagasaki, eventually prompting Victory in Japan Day (VJ Day), observed on August 14, 1945, with the surrender of Japan.

By May 1945, Indianapolis newspapers were carrying the happy news that veterans with enough service points were beginning to be "mustered out" of active duty in earnest via Camp Atterbury in Johnson County, just south of Indianapolis. Three hundred men were discharged via the program in the first week, part of 1.3 million military personnel planned to be discharged in 1945–46.

At the same time, Fort Benjamin Harrison in Indianapolis continued to house more than 2,700 members of the military cited for either disciplinary violations or crimes, as well as those charged with mutiny. On May 31, 1945, tensions inside the camp boiled over as prisoners there staged a deadly riot.

Military officials said that the problems started just before 10:00 p.m. when a few prisoners began throwing debris and breaking lights in the barracks and in common areas outside. Guards on duty were unable to quell what was described as a "well-organized," effort and soon small fires were started in a barracks and a separate infirmary building. Eventually, nine buildings were torched and would burn to the ground aided by heavy winds and machine gun fire from the fort's guard towers that kept firefighters at bay.[185]

In the end, one local firefighter was killed from smoke inhalation trying to fight the blazes, and a fort guard was shot and killed by "friendly fire" from a machine gun in a guard tower. The military confirmed one serious injury to "a Negro soldier" and eight minor injuries for prisoners, all treated at the base hospital.[186]

The story of the riot gained national attention, a rare bit of bad news amid a growing sense that America and its allies had won the war. *Time* magazine described the men at Fort Harrison as "Army recalcitrants and out-and-out criminals: everything from AWOLs to arsonists, rapists and murderers."[187]

An investigation revealed that the prisoners rioted as national news continued to discuss the release of Private Joseph McGee of Massachusetts, who had served time for the alleged abuse of nine Nazi prisoners in Europe. "To the Fort Harrison prisoners, Private McGee was just another, if slightly luckier, guy," *Time* reported. "Cried they: 'If McGee got out, why shouldn't we?'"[188]

Colonel Peyton C. Winlock, commander of the Fort Harrison post, reportedly tried to reason with the men but was struck by a large rock and knocked nearly unconscious. From there, the melee took off, with "prisoners, dodging around the landscaped grounds, trying to skin under the double rows of high-barbed wire fences. Finally, guards blazed away with submachine guns."[189]

"To put down the riot, guards herded the prisoners into groups in the corners of the compound and forced them to lie prone with their arms outstretched," the *Indianapolis News* reported.[190] Eventually, one thousand active duty Fort Harrison troops surrounded the camp "armed with clubs, rifles, automatic rifles, sub-machine guns and .40 caliber pistols," and no prisoners escaped. The riot ended about two hours after it had started.[191]

Fire damages topped $100,000—the firefighting significantly complicated by the fact that firefighters had to spray water from beyond two sets of barbed-wire fences at the compound, and not until the military permitted them to do so.

The *Indianapolis Times* reported that "thousands" of civilians packed East Fifty-sixth Street (then known as Aultman Avenue), Post Road and other nearby streets trying to find out the cause of the huge ball of flames illuminating the night sky. "Military police closed off the fort roads and kept traffic moving as the area was under gunfire," the *Times* reported. "Military guards thrown about the stockade crowded low as the heavy firing broke out."[192] The *Times* also quoted an "overseas veteran" who was now stationed at Fort Harrison as saying, bitterly, "We fought the enemy overseas, and now we gotta fight these guys."[193]

Days later, local reaction remained strong as the Indianapolis Chamber of Commerce openly pressured U.S. Representative Louis Ludlow (1873–1950), an Indianapolis Democrat, to do all he could to get the prison barracks out of Fort Harrison.

The chamber wrote to Representative Ludlow that the riot affirmed their question of "why an army penitentiary should be established so close to a city, [and] particularly why it should be a major function of the long-founded Fort Harrison."[194]

Chamber officials and Representative Ludlow pushed for the induction center that was once housed at Fort Harrison be returned there (from Camp

U.S. Representative Louis Ludlow, circa 1937. *Library of Congress LC-H22-D-649.*

Atterbury, where it was moved in 1944). The military, prone to do what it wanted, did not remove the camp for deserters for many years.

In May 1951, military officials made Indianapolis locals a lot happier with their announcement of plans to construct a $20 million Army Finance Center at Fort Harrison—operating today as DFAS (Defense Finance and Accounting Services).

Tragedy struck the fort one more time, in December 1990, as an explosion fueled by a natural gas leak ripped through a military family housing unit at the fort, killing a five-year-old girl and injuring nineteen others, five critically. The blast at 9:15 p.m. occurred in a four-unit housing complex along Drumm Drive on the west edge of Fort Harrison.

Firefighters had visited the Harrison Village apartments earlier in the day after a complaint of a possible gas leak, and officials from Citizens Gas shut off gas for 240 units in the complex. What they could not know is that the leak was actually in a separate set of apartments, about three hundred yards from where the gas was shut off. Partial evacuation had not been focused on the area that eventually was leveled.

Fort Harrison was decommissioned in 1996 upon the recommendation of the Base Realignment and Closure Commission.

THE GREATEST SPECTACLE IN TRAGEDY?

While the world-famous Indianapolis 500 has forever claimed itself as "the greatest spectacle in racing" and still holds the record as the world's largest single-day sporting event, many noteworthy tragedies have occurred.

In all, since the start of the race one hundred years ago in 1911, sixty-six people have been killed: drivers in the race, drivers killed during practice or race qualifications, crew members of racers, mechanics in practice, crew personnel during the race and spectators. It is perhaps not altogether surprising that the push for speed and the continual advancement of racing equipment has also come with greater risk. Deaths related to the race, however, have slowed dramatically in the last several decades as the design of Indy cars has further emphasized safety.

The deadliest race took place in 1973, when three people were killed on "Pole Day" and "Race Day" combined. A dozen spectators were also badly injured.

The trouble started on Pole Day on May 17, 1973, when driver Art Pollard (1927–1973), a two-time Indy 500 winner, died in a crash. His car slammed into the unforgiving Indianapolis Motor Speedway wall in Turn 1, flipped and killed Pollard. Pollard had been clocked at 192 miles per hour in the lap just before his crash.

When race day finally arrived, unrelenting rain showers delayed the start. The 1973 race was scheduled to start to Memorial Day, Monday, May 28. However, on the opening lap, a crash by driver David "Salt" Walther sent his car and burning racing fuel spewing into the grandstand, injuring eleven fans. Twelve other cars were damaged and could not continue. The track and wall were damaged severely, along with a large portion of the field out on Lap 1, and race officials called the proceedings off until the next day, Tuesday, May 29. That day, only two laps were completed before heavy rain again "red flagged" the proceedings.

The race finally got underway in earnest on Wednesday, May 30, before a greatly reduced crowd, but a crash on Lap 57 spelled more tragedy. The fiery crash in Turn 4 with driver David "Swede" Savage (1946–1973) brought out the track's emergency crew. Moments after the crash, a crew member named Armando Teran began running north toward the crash site from Pit Row and was struck and killed instantly by an emergency crew truck traveling sixty miles per hour. Savage also died from his injuries, weeks later on July 2, 1973.

The race continued until Lap 129, when heavy rain again began falling. Indy 500 officials had had enough—the race was called with just 332.5 of the 500 miles completed, and Gordon Johncock was declared the winner. Johncock would go on to win the 1982 race as well, in the closest finish in 500 history—a 0.16-second win over eventual four-time Indy 500 winner, Rick Mears.

Before 1973, some of the other notable deadly occurrences included the following:

- The 1909 race brought not only the death of driver William "Billy" Borque (1879–1909) but also the death of two spectators.
- In 1919, two drivers, Louis LeCocq (1892–1919) and Arthur Thurman (1879–1919) were killed during the race. LeCocq and his onboard mechanic, Robert Bandini, were killed when the fuel tank

on their racer exploded. Thurman crashed on Lap 44 and died. His onboard mechanic was critically injured but survived.

- The 1933 race had two drivers killed: Mark Billman (1905–1933) and Lester Spangler (1906–1933). Billman died in a crash on Lap 79, while Spangler and his onboard mechanic, Bob Hurst, were killed in a crash on Lap 132. A racing crew member, G.L. Gordon, also died during the 1933 race. That same year, driver William Denver was killed during his third lap trying to qualify his car for the race.

- The 1935 race remained a deadly affair, despite the addition of new safety measures such as crash helmets for the drivers and their onboard mechanics, and green, yellow and red safety lights along the track. Two drivers, rookie driver Johnny Hannon and Hartford "Stubby" Stubblefield (1909–1935), died in qualifications for the race. Both drivers sent their cars over the racetrack wall—Hannon on his first lap at race speed. Stubblefield and his onboard mechanic, Leo Whitaker, were both killed when thrown from their car. During the race itself, driver Clay Weatherly (1910–1935) died in a crash on just the ninth lap of the race.

- Tragedy at the 1955 race deprived popular driver Bill Vokovich (1918–1955) of his third consecutive Indy 500 title when he crashed on Lap 57 of the race on the back straightaway of the track while in first place. Another driver, Manuel Ayulo (1921–1955), also died in qualifications for the race.

- In 1960, events off the track made more headlines than on as a "makeshift scaffold grandstand" collapsed during the pace lap of the race. Two spectators were killed and eighty-two others injured as the scaffold came down almost in slow motion. "Situated just inside a fence that keeps spectators off the grass track apron, the seven-tier scaffold began its slow-motion plunge as the race cars came into view," reported the *Indianapolis Star.* As emergency crews went to the aid of the dead and injured, the race went on. "Some of us tried to help, but primarily people were just interested in watching the race," said eyewitness Nick Longworth, a Fort Wayne news reporter. "There was beer and fried chicken all over the place and they just kept on with it."[195]

- The 1964 race brought perhaps the most spectacular and gruesome crash in 500 history, as drivers Eddie Sachs (1927–1964) and Dave MacDonald (1936–1964) were both burned to death in an inferno in Turn 4. The incredible blaze resulting from the crash led to the eventual switch from gasoline to methanol fuel.

- Finally, in 1971, a bizarre event occurred that resulted in no deaths, but twenty-two reporters and photographers were injured. Local car dealer Eldon Palmer was driving the 1971 pace car that year, a '71 Dodge Challenger. As Palmer entered Pit Row and the drivers began the race, he eventually lost control of the car, crashing into a grandstand. In the pace car with him were Speedway owner Tony Hulman (1901–1977), ABC sportscaster Chris Schenkel (1923–2005) and former astronaut John Glenn. No one inside the pace car was injured, and the race continued as normal.

THE FINAL ACT: A DEADLY BLAST KILLS SEVENTY-FOUR

As the 1964 *Holiday on Ice* show came to its conclusion just moments after 11:00 p.m. on Halloween night, 1963, an incredible blast ripped open a geyser in aisle 13 at the southern end of the Indiana State Fairgrounds Coliseum, sending a wall of flames and a shower of debris down on the crowd.

"A huge, yellowish orange flame shot up from the gaping, jagged crater the blast had created in the area where people had been enjoying themselves seconds earlier," detailed the *Indianapolis Star*.[196]

The devastation was incredible—seventy-four people killed, more than three hundred injured—but miraculously, the majority of the more than four thousand people inside the arena escaped frightened but unharmed.

As *Star* reporter Bill Roberts wrote in a first-person account the day after, "For a few seconds, no one cried out. Everybody seemed stunned. Possibly it was too much for the brain to grasp in a flash. Then, there were screams and cries of agony and the audience jumped from their seats as if in unison and started rushing for the exits. The orchestra continued to play."[197]

It was a disaster of a magnitude the city of Indianapolis had never witnessed before. The death toll was so great, in fact, that Marion County

Indiana State Fairgrounds Coliseum (now known as Pepsi Coliseum). *Photo by Steve Polston.*

coroner Dennis Nicholas used the ice rink in place for the skating show as a temporary morgue for the gruesome task of identifying the sixty-five people killed on the night of the blast. Another nine people would die from their injuries in the weeks and months following the disaster.

All of the victims died of either massive blunt-force injury from being propelled into the air or buried in concrete or from burns inflicted by the gas-fed inferno that briefly engulfed part of the coliseum.

As it became clear how many people were missing in the rubble and presumed dead, the coroner led shocked and grieving family members through the rows of bodies lining the ice rink in order to properly identify the victims.

A lengthy investigation was undertaken that eventually revealed that propane tanks used to heat popcorn in concession stands underneath the grandstand had leaked via a faulty valve.

As expected, among the dead were many children and family members who had come to Indianapolis that evening—forgoing traditional trick-or-treating back home—to get an early start on the holiday season. Eighteen families lost two or more members in the blast. It was the opening night of the show, which never reopened because of the extensive damage to the arena.[198]

Infamous Disasters

As *Time* magazine reported:

> *A chorus line of 36 barelegged beauties on skates swirled in synchronized precision over the ice rink in Indianapolis' State Fairgrounds Coliseum. They wore sequined leotards and yellow-feathered headdresses, and they dipped and swooped together to the ricky-tick tempo of an 18-piece band playing Dixieland. Fireworks sparked near the roof girders, and a family-trade crowd of 4,320 oohed and aahed. This was the finale of the Holiday on Ice show's first night in Indianapolis—a Mardi Gras production number. Before it ended, an explosion thundered through the auditorium. A 30-ft. wall of flame shot over a section of box seats and rinkside folding chairs. In an instant, the rink was littered with enormous chunks of concrete, shredded programs, crumpled popcorn boxes, splintered seats, twisted steel—and dozens of limp or painfully writhing bodies that lay in puddles of blood spreading over the ice. It took a moment for the horror to register. Then the gay chorus line broke in a scramble of skate blades and screams. A woman in the audience shrieked to her companion: "It's part of the show! It's got to be! It's got to be!" The band continued to play Dixieland.*[199]

Reports from the scene indicated bleeding and dazed spectators wandering around outside the coliseum—lucky to have escaped—but many traumatized by trying to find missing members of their party. One man was described as walking aimlessly through the mass asking everyone who passed, "Where's my kids? Where's my kids?"[200]

Initially overwhelmed, Indianapolis police and fire officials gained control of the situation with the added help of the Indiana State Police and the Marion County Sheriff's Department. Local hospitals were jammed with the long line of victims—triage methods being employed so they could treat the most seriously injured first—while the others waited.

In December 1963, a Marion County Grand Jury indicted several persons as a result of the blast, including the state's fire marshal and the Indianapolis fire chief, on misdemeanor charges alleging that the men failed in their duties to properly inspect the fairgrounds facility before the show. Five others were charged with felony manslaughter, including the arena's manager, the concession manager and the suppliers of the propane gas tanks found to have faulty valves.

In its report, the grand jury noted that "explosions just don't happen, they are caused." They focused particularly on propane gas that, because of its volatility, "demands some control which, of course, requires genuine surveillance on the industry to guarantee that the desire for profit on the part of a few will never again relegate the matter of public safety to a point of reckless indifference." They lamented the fact that people responsible for public safety had been "impelled by the profit from the sale…without regard for the safety of persons."[201]

Only one conviction was ever obtained, that of Edward J. Fanger, president of the Discount Gas Corporation, on a charge of assault and battery. The Indiana Supreme Court, however, later tossed the verdict. Civil lawsuits, as expected, quickly piled up, and reports indicated that surviving victims and families of those who died collected about $4.6 million in settlements.[202]

The Coliseum, now known as the Pepsi Coliseum, was closed for just forty-one days after the blast. Repairs were quickly made, and the arena was reopened on December 12, 1963, for a cattle show. The *Holiday on Ice* show returned in November 1964—just one year after the blast—and ticket sales remained strong, with more than 5,000 fans showing up for opening night and 43,328 paying admission for the show's entire run that year.[203]

THE LETHAL SKIES ABOVE INDY

Air travel continued to grow in popularity throughout the 1950s and 1960s, and Hoosiers were not left out of the equation.

Weir Cook Municipal Airport (later renamed Indianapolis International Airport) was the center point of dozens of flights into and out of Indiana every day. Next to Chicago, Cincinnati, Louisville or Detroit, it was the best bet for Indiana residents wanting or needing air travel.

A Deadly Final Approach to Indy

On September 9, 1969, Allegheny Airlines Flight 853 met its moment with infamy over a Shelby County farm field. The flight, carrying seventy-eight passengers and a flight crew of four, was on its final approach to Indianapolis when it plummeted to the earth, narrowly missing the Shady Acres Mobile

Home Park just outside Fairland, Indiana. All aboard the plane perished, as did thirty-four-year-old Robert W. Carey of Indianapolis, a student pilot whose Piper Cherokee 140—a single-engine piston-powered plane—sliced through the rear section of the massive Allegheny DC-9 jet, bringing both craft to the ground.

Witnesses told investigators that Carey's small plane appeared to not see the jet as it flew southward and clipped the northwest bound jet.

"Many watched in horror as parts of bodies and wreckage and broken suitcases plummeted," reported the *Indianapolis Star*. "Some of the bodies and wreckage landed in the mobile homes court."[204]

No one was injured on the ground at Shady Acres, but windows in several of the fifty-three mobile homes in the park were blown out, and "a large oxygen tank from the jet crashed through the roof of one trailer, barely missing a 5-week-old girl being diapered by her mother," the *Star* reported.

Allegheny Flight 853, scheduled to arrive at Weir Cook at 3:39 p.m., had originated in Boston, with quick stopovers in Baltimore and Cincinnati before heading for Indianapolis. The same flight would never make its final leg from Indianapolis to St. Louis.

Ironically, the DC-9 was piloted by an Indiana resident, Captain Jams M. Elrod, a forty-seven-year-old husband and father from Plainfield, Indiana, and a veteran nineteen-year employee of Allegheny Airlines.

Air traffic controllers at Indianapolis reported nothing unusual with the DC-9 prior to it dropping from the "radar scope" at 3:31 p.m. as it descended from 6,000 feet to 2,500 feet as part of its final approach to Indianapolis.

FAA officials were quick to point out that the smaller single-engine plane had not shown up on the radar screens at the Indianapolis airport and that "all transmissions [from the DC-9] were normal…it was near perfect weather," John Shaffer, administrator of the Federal Aviation Administration, told reporters. "It's almost inconceivable that the two planes were in the same spot at the same time."[205]

Neither plane burned upon impact, though witnesses reported that the impact of the two planes sounded like an explosion. On the ground, the DC-9 bore a deep gash in a soybean field adjacent to Interstate 74 estimated to be ten feet deep and came to rest just fifty yards short of the trailer park. The single-engine plane crashed about a mile east of the site, near the railroad tracks leading to Shelbyville.

"Bits of wreckage, bodies and luggage scattered over an area more than 200 yards in radius," reported the *Star*. A grisly detail was added: state and local police gathered up severed fingers found in the wreckage to use for possible fingerprint identification of the victims. "Not one single body was found in the wreckage," police said.[206]

"Pieces flew everywhere," said witness Norman W. Bannett of Fairland. "The back end fell off the passenger plane, it turned over, nose-down, and dropped to the ground. Bits of fuselage, people and fuel were sprayed over a large area."[207]

Another witness, James R. deHoney of Fairland, said that he saw the large pieces of the passenger jet floating to the ground but grew confused about other pieces. "There were strange looking objects, like bodies, falling through the air," deHoney said.[208]

Debris was spread across a wide area of more than five thousand feet in four directions, with residents of Shady Acres notifying police of "parts of bodies" and "clothing hanging from trees and along fences in the soybean field."[209]

Carey's flight, ironically his first solo flight ever as he completed his student pilot training, had originated from the Brookside Airport near McCordsville, Indiana, a small community northeast of Indianapolis. He was assigned to fly from Brookside to the Bakalar Air Force Base near Columbus, Indiana, and return to Brookside.

As body parts were recovered, Indiana State Police and Shelby County Sheriff's Department officers set up a makeshift morgue inside the Indiana National Guard Armory in Shelbyville. There a crowd of families and the curious continued to grow as news soon came—there were no survivors.

That news also arrived at the Allegheny terminal inside Weir Cook Airport as friends and families waited on passengers to arrive. Reporter Thomas M. Keating of the *Indianapolis Star* reported that the airport "seemed to slow down in a state of shock. Planes arrived and departed and people came and went, but everybody by then was aware that the 35 persons sitting and standing around the Allegheny Airlines passenger boarding area were waiting for a plane that never would arrive."[210]

"They're not coming, they're not coming," sobbed a lone woman identified as Mrs. James Alexander of Danville, Illinois. She had driven to Indianapolis to retrieve her parents, Mr. and Mrs. Robert Young of Baltimore, who were passengers on Flight 853.

Detroit attorney Henry Gage was among those waiting for the flight, but his plans were to board it to get to St. Louis. Gage said that he had used Flight 853 many times, telling reporters it was "a businessman's flight."[211] Gage said that the crash did not deter him from flying, noting that "you never know when your time is up" and that he still saw air travel as "the only way to go."[212]

The investigation into the crash of Flight 853 was immediately clouded by allegations raised by the National Association of Government Employees (NAGE) that radar coverage of the crash site was inadequate. Further, critics claimed that the FAA had been informed of this shortfall months before the crash but had not addressed it—a charge federal officials denied.

"There is no question that our radar equipment [at Weir Cook] is the best available today," said Duane L. Jennings, chief controller for the FAA at Indianapolis. "It is as good as the equipment that is being used at Kennedy or Los Angeles international airports."[213]

The National Transportation Safety Board issued its report on the crash on July 15, 1970, noting that the visibility at the time of the crash was at least fifteen miles (a critical fact since the student pilot was using only visual flight rules), "but there was an intervening cloud condition which precluded the crew of either aircraft from sighting the other until a few seconds prior to collision."[214]

The NTSB said that it had determined "the probable cause of this accident to be the deficiencies in the collision avoidance capability of the traffic control system" at Indianapolis. "The deficiencies included the inadequacy of the see-and-avoid concept under circumstances of this case; the technical limitations of radar in detecting all aircraft; and the absence of Federal Aviation Regulations which would provide a system of adequate separation of mixed visual-flight rules and instrument-flight rules traffic in the terminal area."[215]

The plane's mechanical and voice flight recorders were recovered, damaged but still usable. They revealed nothing unusual prior to the plane suddenly losing speed and altitude, as well as one line from pilot Elrod declaring just seconds after 3:29 p.m., "I'm going down."

"Radar has proven itself a safe and efficient tool for the positive control of air traffic," the NTSB concluded. "However, in this incident it is believed that two independent radar systems failed to detect the presence of [the smaller plan], and as a result, no warning was given to the crew of Allegheny 953 regarding the specific direction of the hazard. Had the crew been provided with this information, their chances of seeing and avoiding the other aircraft below the cloud layer would have been enhanced."[216]

Ramada Inn Fighter Jet Crash

Just after 9:00 a.m. on Tuesday, October 20, 1987, air traffic controllers at Indianapolis International Airport received a transmission from U.S. Air Force major Bruce L. Teagarden that the engine of his A-7D Corsair II had failed and that he needed to make an immediate emergency landing. Teagarden's plane was fifteen miles south of the airport at the time and approached the airport's main north–south runway at an estimated altitude of 3,100 feet—far too high to make a safe landing.

Teagarden, thirty-five, attempted to glide the plane over the airport's main east–west runway and make a second attempt to land the powerless plane. He didn't succeed. Air traffic controllers reported that the plane dropped from their radar at 1,300 feet, and at about 500 feet, Teagarden activated the pilot's ejection system as the plane veered violently out of control and to the east of the Indianapolis airport terminal.

Just after ejecting, Teagarden's plane clipped the top of a Bank One branch building at the corner of Bradbury Street and Executive Drive, east of the interchange of I-465 and the Airport Expressway. Seconds later, the plane careened up an embankment and became slightly airborne again before violently sliding under the front entrance canopy of the seven-story Ramada Inn Airport Hotel. The jet finally came to rest seventy-five feet inside the lobby of the hotel—spewing and igniting deadly jet fuel.

"The aircraft shattered into many pieces, sending the cockpit and engine into the lobby and its wings to the top of the carport and upper floors of the hotel, simultaneously igniting its approximately 20,000 lbs. of fuel," noted a final report from the U.S. Fire Services Division of the Federal Emergency Management Agency (FEMA).[217]

Nine people, all hotel employees, were killed—four burned beyond recognition as jet fuel exploded inside the hotel. Four others were injured, including the pilot, another hotel employee, a hotel guest and a man who had stopped briefly at the hotel to use the pay phone inside. Teagarden's ejection saved his life, as he landed in the parking lot of a supply company just west of the crash site with non-life-threatening injuries.

The surviving but injured hotel worker, Betty Gonzales, fifty-two, was in the laundry room adjacent to the front lobby and escaped through heavy smoke to an outside exit. Her colleagues who remained behind in the laundry room all died. The only hotel guest injured suffered minor burns and a broken leg as he jumped from his room to the roof of the hotel's kitchen outside his window.

Most seriously injured among the survivors was Tom Murray, forty-one, who suffered burns to 95 percent of his body. He had just completed his telephone call inside the hotel lobby and was returning to his car in the parking lot outside when the plane careened into the building.

Those killed were Christopher L. Evans, twenty-one; Allen Mantor, eighteen; Brenda J. Henry, twenty-six; Katherine Cox, thirty-three; Beth L. Goldberg, thirty; Emma J. Brownlee, thirty-seven; Narinda S. Kanwar, forty-one; Dawn Martin, nineteen; and Mary Marsh, twenty-nine.

Evans's family told reporters that he called his mother moments after the crash. "Mom, I think I'm going to be OK," his mother Barbara Evans quoted him as saying moments before the line went dead.[218]

"The A-7 is 48 feet long and 34 feet wide," the U.S. Fire Service report indicated. "Its wings severed from the main body of the aircraft, slamming into an area of the building just above the carport, blowing small pieces of metal through the windows of several rooms, and simultaneously igniting the remaining fuel stored in multiple areas of the aircraft. A giant fireball momentarily engulfed the entire outside front of the hotel to about the fourth floor."[219]

The plane, a military jet fighter, had departed earlier that morning from Pittsburgh International Airport and was operated by the Pennsylvania Air National Guard. Military officials reported that the jet had passed a lengthy preflight inspection less than twenty-four hours before the crash.

Witnesses said that Teagarden was disoriented once he landed on the ground, asking more than once what city he was in. He was able to walk and was led to a telephone to call both his wife and his superior officer.[220]

The night before the crash, 130 guests were registered in the Ramada's 165 rooms, typical for a weekday at the busy facility. However, by the time of the crash, more than half of those guests had already checked out. All of the guests on the upper floors of the hotel were able to safely evacuate by avoiding the front lobby and before flames briefly spread up the hotel's front façade.

While it only took firefighters a few minutes to extinguish the fire, its effects were devastating. As firefighters searched the building and confirmed that all guests had successfully exited the hotel via other fire exits, a grim discovery lay before them.

"Three bodies were found in an area behind the reception desk on the first floor," FEMA reported. "Another body was found in an office behind the reception area. Two [additional] bodies were found in an office off the lobby area. Three bodies were found in the laundry room, located down the hall from the lobby. All fatalities were later identified as employees of the hotel."[221] Of the nine fatalities, four were burned beyond recognition and were identified using medical and dental records. "The remaining five died essentially from smoke inhalation and some thermal burns," noted the federal report.[222]

Following the crash and investigation, some criticism was raised about the pilot, Teagarden, and how he had handled the disabled craft. He maintained that he had tried to find an open area to dump the craft, but it is believed that the downdraft created by the activation of the pilot ejection seat had forced the plane off course and toward the Ramada Inn.

Teagarden cooperated fully with investigators and issued a written public statement that he hoped would reassure some doubters and help heal some of the pain: "It is impossible to express to you how deeply grieved I am by your loss," Teagarden wrote.[223] "I wish with all my heart that it had been within my power to keep my plane headed toward that open field once I aimed it there...Please understand that I did everything humanly possible to prevent this. My prayers are with all of [of the victims' loved ones]."[224]

The Tragedy of Flight 4184

For decades, O'Hare International Airport in Chicago has been listed as the nation's busiest airport, each day handling more than 2,400 flights and nearly 1 million flights per year. Not surprisingly, almost anyone who has flown into or out of Chicago has experienced a delay.

Delay was the name of the game on Halloween night, October 31, 1994, as American Eagle Flight 4184, a regular commuter flight from Indianapolis, was told by air controllers at O'Hare that it would have to wait. In fact, Flight 4184 would circle in a driving autumn rainstorm for thirty-two minutes over the counties of northwest Indiana, southeast of Chicago (one of eleven flights that night waiting for the OK to land).

Finally cleared for landing, 4184 began its descent from the ten thousand feet at which it had been circling to eight thousand feet. Within moments, however, it dropped from the radar at O'Hare, and the flight and all sixty-eight of its passengers and crew would be lost to the ages.

The flight ended in a vacant farm field just outside Roselawn, Indiana, a town better known for its two nudist camps, the Ponderosa Sun Club and Naked City. Officials from both Newton and Jasper Counties responded as the crash occurred adjacent to the county line. What they found was nothing.

Although blackened by nightfall, fog and heavy rain, initial responders reported the almost unbelievable: There was nothing left of Flight 4184. Most pieces of debris found were no larger than a person's hand.

"It was mass devastation out there on the scene," Indiana State Police trooper Pat King said.[225] Fellow trooper Larry Bartley told a reporter, "Don't ask me to describe [the scene]. It would make you sick to your stomach."[226]

Farmer Norm Prohosky and his hired man, Robert Hilton, both witnessed the crash, telling investigators that the plane plunged into the ground at a ninety-degree angle. "The way it hit, I thought, 'Oh God.' It's a hell of a weird feeling because you knew that there would be no survivors," Hilton said.[227] It was a conclusion that investigators from the National Transportation Safety Board (NTSB) confirmed.

"The plane was extremely fractured, fragmented in the impact," NTSB spokesman Ted Lopatkiewicz told reporters. He said that the crash site was extremely muddy and that the site had been declared "a biohazard because of all the human tissue. Investigators cannot go in unless they are wearing proper suits. That makes it a more arduous task than it [otherwise] would be."[228]

NTSB investigators did locate the plane's cockpit data and voice recorders, as well as a six- by eight-foot piece of the plane's tail that remained intact above a huge crater in the field. Investigators called in police dogs to help find miniscule body parts such as teeth, fillings or dentures to help identify victims. Among the sixty-eight casualties, twelve Hoosiers were killed.

The crash highlighted complaints that many passengers and airline industry watchdogs had raised for years: should flights expected to be delayed upon reaching their destination be kept holding in the air near the destination airport or just kept on the ground at their point of origination? Flight 4184 *had* been delayed from its original departure from Indianapolis because of deteriorating conditions at Chicago but eventually was cleared to fly. That didn't prevent the need for an additional in-flight delay for 4184.

Months of investigation followed, with federal investigators declaring that a ridge of ice had built up on the wings of the plane while it was in a holding pattern waiting to land in Chicago. "The ice buildup caused the autopilot to disengage which caused the plane to bank to the right and roll over," reported the *Indianapolis Star*. The NTSB termed it "an uncommanded roll."[229]

Two years later, a full NTSB report absolved the flight crew of any error, instead blaming ATR, the French builder of the turboprop ATR-72, and French aviation authorities. French authorities disputed those findings, blaming the flight crew. Review of flight recorders did indicate that the plane's pilot had left the cockpit for several minutes to socialize with a flight attendant in the moments before the plane lost control.

In 2002, the NTSB updated its final report on the crash. "The plane's European manufacturer and French aviation officials had petitioned the safety board to drop its criticisms that they had known of or failed to communicate problems about the ATR-72," the Associated Press reported.[230]

The AP added that "Avions de Transport Regional (ATR), the manufacturer, said it disagreed with the conclusion that it had known the plane had a history of accumulating ice on its wings that could cause instability in the ailerons, movable parts that guide an aircraft's lateral movement."[231]

Seven years after the crash, a letter and package arrived at the suburban Indianapolis home of Jennifer Stansberry-Miller, sister of crash victim Brad Stansberry. In it were Brad's driver's license, his work identification card and a credit card.

"Honest to God, my mouth fell to the floor and I could not speak," Stansberry-Miller said. "I was absolutely dumbfounded. Blown away."[232]

American Airlines officials said that they had located Brad's belongings in an airline storage area in Texas in 1999, five years after the crash, but had waited to turn the materials over to the next of kin.[233]

Part IV
Infamous Politicians

HOOSIER CONGRESSMEN IN THE HOT SEAT

Two members of Indiana's Congressional delegation have faced severe rebuke from their colleagues in the U.S. House of Representatives and the U.S. Senate—one resulting in a rare censure and the other in an even rarer expulsion.

Senator Jesse D. Bright (1812–1875) first came to Indianapolis as a state senator representing Jefferson County in far southern Indiana. He soon became a star of the Democratic Party and in 1842 was elected lieutenant governor of Indiana. His political capital continued to rise as he was named to a seat in the U.S. Senate in 1844 just as his term as lieutenant governor was coming to an end.

It was during the onset of the Civil War that a Republican majority in the U.S. Senate began to carefully scrutinize the statements and perceived loyalties of their Democratic colleagues—most especially "butternut Democrats" from southern Indiana such as Bright. Although Indiana was a Union state, there remained strong opinions opposing the abolition of slavery and equally strong opinions opposing the federal government's role in telling Southern states what to do.

Bright was openly anti-abolitionist but seemed to place it in the context of supporting a state's own right to govern itself. He was one of a number of Democrats who tended to look the other way regarding slavery and desperately wanted to avoid a civil war between the North and the South.

Regardless, as the Civil War commenced, Bright's actions came under scrutiny until, on December 16, 1861, Senator Morton S. Wilkinson (1819–1894), a Republican from Minnesota, presented to his fellow senators what he considered an incriminating letter written by Senator Bright. The letter, dated March 1, 1861, consisted of an introduction of Bright's Madison, Indiana colleague Thomas A. Lincoln and indicated that Lincoln could be of help in obtaining firearms and other munitions. The troubling fact was that the letter was addressed to "His Excellency Jefferson Davis, President of the Confederation of States." Senator Wilkinson and many others believed that Bright's letter "was evidence of disloyalty to the United States, and is calculated to give aid and comfort to the public enemies."[234]

Senator Bright gave an impassioned speech in which he declared that "every impulse of my heart, and every tie that binds me to earth, is interwoven with the form of government under which we live, and to which I acknowledge my allegiance, and I will yield to no man in my attachment to it."[235] He added, "And though I have been assailed with all of the fury of party spirit, and my character unjustly aspersed, and my loyalty and devotion questioned, this shall not alienate me from the faith of my life, or lessen the great obligation I feel. I have devoted the humble energies of my life to the support of the government under which we live, and which I would not exchange for any other on earth."[236]

Despite his statements of loyalty, Wilkinson's motion to expel Bright from the Senate was passed thirty-two to fourteen after a lengthy and emotional debate. As part of his expulsion, the federal government seized Bright's property in Jefferson County, Indiana, to be used as a Union hospital.

Indiana's Senator Bright would earn the distinction of being the last United States senator expelled in history. Afterward, Bright relocated unrepentant to Kentucky (later being elected to that state's legislature).

Another Hoosier suffered the shame of having been in the small group of congressmen ever censured—although the circumstances of the case tended to make Congressman William D. Bynum (1846–1927) of Indianapolis a hero among Democrats across the nation.

A one-time Speaker of the Indiana House of Representatives, during his five-term tenure in the U.S. House between 1885 and 1895, Bynum continued to win leadership roles, at one time serving as the Democratic minority whip.

U.S. Senator William
D. Bynum. *Library
of Congress LC-H25-
110434-L.*

Bynum's troubles arose in May 1890 when he described a fellow representative, a Pennsylvania Republican, as a "liar and a perjurer."[237]

A fierce debate raged on the House floor as to whether Congressman Bynum's comments were worthy of expulsion from the Congress, until a resolution was reached by which Bynum accepted a censure from the Republican leadership. He did so, however, flanked by the 104 Democratic members of the House, who crowded into the well of the House chambers with him.

Addressing his fellow members of Congress, Bynum offered a rather obtuse apology, of sorts, which came at the end of proceedings that some believed would result in the Hoosier congressman being expelled. After the censure was read, Bynum told the Speaker, "I accept the censure of the House as a decoration of honor."[238]

Bynum's original remarks that started the fracas would be considered tame by some standards today. At the time, however, they were described as "astonishing," "offensive" and "far beneath the dignity of any legislative body" and produced "an acrimonious fire between Republicans and Democrats."[239]

Bynum won just one additional term in Congress in 1892, failing in his reelection bid in 1894. In 1900, President William McKinley (1843–1901) appointed Bynum as a Democratic representative to a federal commission on codifying federal statutes. He also gained fame as a leader of the national Democratic Party and served two years as its chairman. He eventually returned to a quiet life in Indianapolis, where he died in 1927.

CLEVELAND AND HENDRICKS: A SHORT-LIVED "PARTNERSHIP"

Thomas A. Hendricks (1819–1885) of Indiana was elected vice president of the United States in 1884 more out of happenstance than real desire to serve. Hendricks had been a compromise choice for deeply divided Democrats seeking a running mate for Governor Grover Cleveland (1837–1908) of New York. Hendricks had previously sought the office in earnest in the election of 1876, running with Samuel Tilden (1814–1886). He ran for president himself once, failing to gain the Democratic nomination. He had previously served two terms in the U.S. Senate from Indiana, plus one term as governor of Indiana.

His curious rise to the vice presidency, however, came without him ever having met Cleveland before their election. Both men were sworn into office on March 4, 1885, and promptly began ignoring each other. Cleveland had no interest in Hendricks and reportedly did not want him on the ticket.[240]

The differences between Hendricks and Cleveland may have started during the campaign, when Hendricks publicly said that he continued to support Governor Cleveland but privately spoke ill of the swirling and eventually confirmed rumors that Cleveland had fathered an illegitimate son. The Cleveland-Hendricks ticket only won the popular vote by a margin of twenty thousand votes—another close win for Hendricks, who began to describe the political process as "very unpleasant."[241]

Cleveland, a bachelor, was apparently also annoyed by reports circulating that Hendricks's wife planned to be the official "host" for White House functions, a report Hendricks had to personally tamp down. Cleveland and Hendricks

A statue of Vice President Thomas A. Hendricks, Indiana Statehouse. *Photo by Steve Polston.*

clashed again—also in public—over political patronage appointments for Democratic Party loyalists. Hendricks complained, "The Democratic Party isn't in power. Grover Cleveland is making a party of his own."[242]

When pressed, Vice President Hendricks made a startling disclosure to reporters that his relations with the president "when we meet are decidedly cordial," but added a zinger: "I have not seen the President in four months, but I have no doubt when I meet him it will be on terms of the most cordial Democratic fellowship."[243]

His chances to meet with the president he served would soon end, as Hendricks died unexpectedly in Indianapolis on November 25, 1885, after attending a reception in his honor. He had served as vice president for less than nine months, the shortest tenure in U.S. history in that office. Interestingly, Cleveland finished his term in office without appointing a new vice president.

MR. HARRISON TAKES A BRIDE

Throughout his very public life, President Benjamin Harrison (1833–1901) of Indiana provided few, if any, scandalous or provocative headlines—that is, until he took a second wife twenty-five years his junior, a woman who was his niece by marriage.

In the years before her January 1948 death, little attention was paid to Mary Scott Lord Harrison, a quiet eighty-nine-year-old widow who enjoyed tea with her friends and weekly mass at the Church of St. Thomas near her home in New York City.

Under a headline proclaiming that she had lived her life in "metropolitan obscurity," the *Indianapolis Times* reported that "[d]eath came today to a woman whom most of the world remembered only as a page in history—Mary Scott Lord Harrison, widow of Benjamin Harrison, 23rd President of the United States."[244]

The *Times* took the occasion of Mrs. Harrison's passing to remind the world that she had once "thrilled the nation" with her "defiant marriage to President Harrison soon after the death of her aunt, [and] his wife."[245] "To the casual observer, she was like any of hundreds of genteel widows with whom she had tea," the *Times* report continued. "Only a few intimates and her family were aware of her role in U.S. history."[246]

Although never First Lady during Harrison's one four-year term as president between 1889 and 1893, she did spend a great deal of time in the White House, caring for her ailing aunt, Caroline Scott Harrison (1832–1892), who had married Benjamin Harrison in 1853.

Caroline Harrison died of complications from pneumonia and tuberculosis in the Lincoln Bedroom of the White House during the early morning hours of October 25, 1892, with her husband and children at her side. Also present was Mrs. Harrison's niece, young Mary. Mary had come to Washington in 1889 "as a girl widow" at the invitation of her aunt, after the young woman was widowed just six months into her first marriage.

After Caroline Harrison's death, hard times continued for the president from Indianapolis, as he lost the 1892 rematch with former president Grover Cleveland (1837–1908) and returned to Indianapolis to resume his law practice.

"To the President, [Mrs. Harrison's] death is an unspeakable loss," reported the *Indianapolis Journal* in 1892. "The bride of his youth, the wife of his mature

Above: President Benjamin Harrison takes the oath of office, March 4, 1889. *Library of Congress LC-USZ62-63418.*

Right: First Lady Caroline Scott Harrison, first wife of President Benjamin Harrison, circa 1889. *Library of Congress LC-USZ62-25798.*

years, the companion of a lifetime, the sharer of his joys and sorrows, his triumphs and defeats, her death leaves him alone in his high place, alone in the performance of weighty duties, alone at morning, noon and at night, alone though surrounded by the pomp and circumstance of office."[247]

The *Journal* added, "Those who know [President Harrison] best know his heart will be torn and shattered by this blow, and how silently and bravely he will bear the grief that cannot be told nor shared. The President will have the sincere sympathy of all Americans."[248]

Mrs. Harrison's Indianapolis funeral on October 28, 1892, was an incredible display, drawing former presidents and vice presidents, cabinet members and thousands of onlookers, who watched the funeral procession carry her to her final rest at Crown Hill Cemetery. It would be a similar show to what the city witnessed in 1901 upon the death of former president Harrison.

In 1896, however, headlines in Indianapolis, Washington and New York carried the happier and exciting news that the former president planned to wed his niece by marriage in a gallant New York City ceremony.

"The marriage caused a great stir because the [two] children of General Harrison staunchly opposed it and refused to attend the ceremony," the *Indianapolis Times* reported. "But newspaper accounts of the wedding are unanimous in commenting on the beauty, proud bearing and distinction of General Harrison's young bride, who took her vows audibly, almost defiantly, before a small group of friends inside St. Thomas."[249]

The *Indianapolis Journal* reported that "Washington society is all agog over the Harrison nuptials in New York." The report included specific details about gifts exchanged between the couple, as well as the wedding dress and traveling dress that the new Mrs. Harrison wore on the train from New York City to Indianapolis.[250]

The couple kept the exact hour of their wedding a secret, although every other detail about their comings and going were widely reported—including reporters who followed the former president to a nearby haberdashery, reporting that he bought a neck tie for one dollar.

One of Harrison's aides, E. Frank Tibbott, told New York reporters that "General Harrison does not want a crowd to be around the church when they go in and out. It is not that he desires to make himself exclusive, but he does not like [his bride-to-be] to be subjected to the eager gaze of people who are not in any way interested in her or in him. It is quite a private matter."[251]

Mary Scott Lord Harrison, second
wife of President Benjamin
Harrison, circa 1914. *Library of
Congress LC-USZ62-25800.*

Grave site of President Benjamin
Harrison, Crown Hill Cemetery.
Photo by Steve Polston.

In the years after President Harrison's death in Indianapolis in 1901, the second Mrs. Harrison returned to New York City, where she lived in growing obscurity. She remained grateful, however, for her five-year marriage to the former president.

"I was a lucky woman," the second Mrs. Harrison told an *Indianapolis Times* reporter in 1936. She said that she was married to "a man whose cultural contacts were so wide and his zest for life was as strong as my own. We met the most interesting personalities of the times, took eight trips abroad, enjoyed plays and concerts and books together."[252]

The second Mrs. Harrison was also buried at Crown Hill Cemetery in Indianapolis, alongside her famous husband and the first Mrs. Harrison, her beloved aunt.

VICE PRESIDENT "COCKTAIL CHARLIE" WARREN FAIRBANKS

Charles Warren Fairbanks (1852–1918) of Indiana made a name for himself in the U.S. Senate as someone who didn't make a lot of waves. Perhaps that is why Republicans believed that he was the perfect contrast to Theodore Roosevelt (1858–1919), who became the nation's twenty-sixth president upon the assassination of President William McKinley (1843–1901).

But as vice president, Fairbanks's image took a different shine—one that did not always please President Roosevelt and perhaps that explains why Roosevelt backed William Howard Taft (1857–1930) as his replacement. During his four-year term as veep, Fairbanks seemingly did little to win the appreciation of Roosevelt.

In 1907, as Indianapolis prepared to roll out all the red, white and blue bunting, the rivalry between Roosevelt and Fairbanks was to play out on Fairbanks's home turf. The president had accepted an invitation to help dedicate a new statute in Indianapolis commemorating the life of Spanish-American War hero General Henry W. Lawson (1843–1899).

The *New York Times* declared in its headlines, "President to Overshadow Vice President in His Own State To-Day." It added, "There are quite a few grins at the predicament of Charles Warren Fairbanks, Vice President, with the President at Indianapolis to-day."[253]

President Theodore Roosevelt and Charles Warren Fairbanks at Roosevelt's home, July 16, 1904, in a photo reflecting the lack of a connection between the two men. *Library of Congress LC-USZ62-7351.*

The Meridian Street home of Vice President Charles Warren Fairbanks. *Photo by Steve Polston.*

"There is a Roosevelt sentiment in Indiana now that is giving the Fairbanks people grave anxiety," the *Times* reported. "Mr. Fairbanks had determined before the dedication of the Lawson monument programme was arranged not to appear again in public with the President."[254]

But Fairbanks had no choice; he not only played second fiddle to President Roosevelt on his home turf but also hosted a high-profile luncheon for the president and other dignitaries in the Fairbanks home at 2960 North Meridian Street. Forty guests gathered for lunch, but "one item on the menu received nationwide attention—Manhattan cocktails."[255]

"A teetoaling Methodist, Fairbanks may not have drank any liquor himself at the luncheon, but he bore the brunt of the nationwide newspaper attacks on his character when they learned of the cocktail incident," wrote historian Ray E. Boomhower. "Already nicknamed 'Buttermilk Charlie' for his advocacy of buttermilk instead of hard liquor, Fairbanks had a brand-new moniker after the affair—'Cocktail Charlie.'"[256]

Privately, it was reported that Roosevelt felt that Fairbanks was getting a raw deal. Publicly, the president did little to save Fairbanks from the brewing controversy and, in fact, quickly jumped behind Taft for the 1908 Republican nomination.

Fairbanks was back on the national ticket one last time in 1916—again as the GOP's vice presidential nominee—but he and Charles Evans Hughes (1862–1948) lost the race to Democrats Woodrow Wilson (1856–1924) and *his* Indiana running mate, Thomas R. Marshall (1854–1925). Fairbanks did help the Republicans carry Indiana, however.

Democratic Party officials at the Indianapolis home of Governor Thomas R. Marshall, August 20, 1912. Marshall is seated at the center of row one. *Library of Congress.*

Charles Warren Fairbanks on a Washington, D.C., street, circa 1916. *Library of Congress LC-H261-6465.*

One final controversy swirled around Fairbanks's name—this time following his death. His daughter, Adelaide F. Timmons, filed a lawsuit accusing her brothers, Frederick C. and Warren C. Fairbanks, of conspiring to steal the remains of their father's estate. The estate was estimated to be worth $8 million, the bulk of which was tied up in $4 million in real estate in Indiana and another reported fifteen thousand acres in Illinois also valued at about $4 million.[257] "The probated will was drafted by my brothers, Frederick and Warren, after my father was so weakened and enfeebled by disease that he was unable to know and comprehend the effect of his acts," Mrs. Timmons said.[258]

Fairbanks's daughter said that she was not upset that she was scheduled to receive only $50,000 cash and a $20,000 annual annuity but rather that her brothers had reduced her father's planned gift to the City of Indianapolis from $500,000 to $50,000. She said that their act had subjected her deceased father to public ridicule once again.

Governor Thomas R. Marshall is notified of his nomination for vice president at an Indianapolis rally on August, 20, 1912. *Library of Congress.*

A ROUGH-AND-TUMBLE START FOR A "TRUE STATESMAN"

Thomas R. Marshall of Indiana gained the admiration and love of his fellow Americans serving as vice president of the United States during an incredibly trying period—one during which an incapacitated President Wilson went virtually unseen by Marshall and the rest of the nation from the time of his stroke in October 1919 until the end of his term in 1921.

It was the start of Marshall's first campaign, however, that provided a big bang, literally. On August 20, 1912, as thousands of Democrats rallied in downtown Indianapolis to celebrate the expected nomination of their fellow Hoosier, Marshall, for vice president, tragedy struck.

"A grandstand directly behind the speaker's platform proved too weak for the crowd which taxed its strength, and it gave way during the exercises," the *New York Times* reported. "Fully one-third of those who went down in the crash were women. The list of injured included state officials and an uncle of Gov. Marshall."[259]

The collapse occurred about ten minutes into the proceedings,

> *when the great stand, 60 feet long and 30 feet wide, swayed twice and then went down to the pavement, carrying with it more than 350 persons… Suddenly a pall of quiet fell across the multitude that had crowded about the*

*corner of New York and Pennsylvania Avenues to witness the notification
of the Indiana Governor. There was a slow, grinding noise, and the speaker
stopped, turning in his tracks to see the crash behind him.*[260]

As "men and women were hurled to the pavement in a tangled mass
of debris," Governor Marshall and Indianapolis mayor Thomas Taggart
(1856–1929) worked to restore order, and panic was avoided. Reporters
described a "seething mass of persons emptied onto the street among the
jagged ends of the rough lumber, as if dumped from a great waste basket,
and it seemed unbelievable that none was killed."[261]

Marshall's term as vice president, however, was less eventful, at least in the
first term. It was during that time when he gained fame for his quote, "What
this country needs is a really good five-cent cigar."

During Wilson's hard-fought second term, however, unprecedented events
would unfold. Wilson, clearly incapacitated and unable to serve, was shielded
from Marshall, members of the cabinet and Congress. Marshall himself did
nothing to force Wilson and his wife and a small circle of advisers to give up
the presidency.

As historian Peter T. Harstad wrote:

*A lesser man might have thrown the country into a constitutional turmoil.
Instead, Marshall used the vice presidency to stabilize the executive branch
and to calm the nation. Operating without precedent during a president's
incapacitation, Marshall conducted affairs of state with dignity. A wise
and kindly man, he deserves the designation* statesman.[262]

After leaving office, more details about the seriousness of Wilson's condition emerged, but Marshall remained loyal. His memoirs were well received after he left office, and he died of a heart attack while visiting Washington, D.C., in 1925. He is buried in Indianapolis.

RIOT-BUSTER RALSTON

Governor Samuel M. Ralston (1857–1925) came to office after winning the 1912 election with a little help from a former Republican, former U.S. senator Albert J. Beveridge (1862–1927), who switched from the GOP to the Progressive Party, giving the Indiana governorship to Ralston and the Democrats.

Ralston's mettle would be tested early as a strike by Indianapolis streetcar workers turned ugly and was followed by a mutiny of a portion of the Indianapolis Police Department, sending the city into violent turmoil. In the end, four people were killed and hundreds more injured in violent clashes that lasted for eight days as the railroad workers fought for improved working conditions.

The problems erupted when the Amalgamated Association of Street and Electric Railway Workers attempted to organize the nine hundred workers of the Indianapolis Traction and Terminal Company. As part of that effort, they called for a general strike by motormen and conductors on October 31, 1913. Among their demands was that Ralston call a special session of the General Assembly to pass laws that protected workers. Ralston initially refused.

In response to the strike that quickly began to cripple the heavily used streetcar system in Indianapolis, the company "dispatched strike breakers to keep the trains running, but violence broke out," according to the *Encyclopedia of Indianapolis*. "Thirty-three IPD officers conducted 'mutiny' when the company asked the city police officers to ride the trains to protect the strike breakers. Only 20 arrests were made, but at least one patrolman resigned instead of riding the train. Another 29 resigned two days later."[263]

Days later, a crowd estimated at more than eight thousand rioters wrecked and burned a streetcar stopped on Illinois Street, just a block from the statehouse, injuring thirty people. After that, Governor Ralston relented

U.S. Senator and former governor Samuel M. Ralston, circa 1922. *Library of Congress LC-F81-21685.*

from his previous position, declared martial law and ordered two thousand Indiana National Guard members to restore order to Indianapolis.

The strikers quickly turned their attention to the statehouse, surrounding it with angry mobs calling for the governor to speak. Ralston did speak to the assembled crowd and promised to assist them in getting certain changes made…*if* they peacefully returned to work.

Eventually, the streetcar company and strikers came to agreeable terms, and the train schedule resumed. Further, Ralston kept his word and pushed Indiana legislators to pass the state's first laws covering minimum wages, working hours, workplace regulations and worker's injury compensation funding.

A NEW DISCLOSURE FROM SENATOR NEW

Harry Stewart New (1858–1937) grew up in Indianapolis and attended Butler University before becoming a reporter (and eventually a co-owner of the *Indianapolis Journal*). He also served as a captain in the Spanish-American War and quickly rose through the ranks of Republican politics in Indianapolis.

New earned his way in an era of Republican dominance in Indianapolis and eventually became a member of the Republican National Committee for twelve years, one year (1907–8) as its president. Back in Indiana, New easily won election to the Indiana General Assembly as a state senator in 1896 and served until 1900.

In 1916, New scored a major upset in defeating U.S. Senator John W. Kern (1849–1917), a Democrat, but served just one term, failing to win the Republican nomination in the 1922 GOP primary. It was likely a parade of nasty headlines and unseemly details from a scandal that erupted in the summer of 1919 that spelled doom for New's senatorial reelection hopes.

On July 6, 1919, the *Indianapolis Star* carried headlines detailing the murder confession of a previously undisclosed son of the sitting senator,

U.S. Senator and Mrs. Harry S. New, circa 1919. *Library of Congress LC-H261-30475.*

thirty-two-year-old Harry S. New Jr. of Glendale, California, who walked into the headquarters of the Los Angeles Police Department personally. The younger New told the desk sergeant that they would find the body of a dead woman inside his car parked out front.

Slumped there, police indeed found Frieda J. Lesser, twenty-one, with whom the young New said he had quarreled earlier during a car ride in Topanga Canyon in rural Los Angeles County. New told investigators that the fight started when Lesser refused to marry him, and he shot her in the head.[264]

For many back in Indianapolis, the news coming from Los Angeles was the first any of them knew that senator New had a son or a reported prior marriage.

Los Angeles detectives quoted New Jr. as saying, "We didn't understand each other, and so I shot her and here I am. There she is too," as he led police to his car to find the body.[265] New said that the shooting ended an otherwise fine day as the young couple took a motor tour of the Venice Beach area, Hollywood, and then to Topanga Canyon. The car belonged to New's mother, identified as Mrs. Lulu M. Burger, also of Glendale, and carried the lifeless woman's body for two hours until New decided to drive to police headquarters to confess and surrender.

Reporters were soon allowed into New's cell at the Los Angeles City Jail, and he told them, "We had planned to be married today. At the last moment, Frieda interposed objections and I proposed that we take an auto ride to some quiet spot where we could talk things over. Reaching a lonely spot, I started pleading with her to marry me at once."[266]

Young New added, "She remained obdurate and said she would resort to any means rather than become my wife. That made me mad. I almost, before I knew it, I had snatched a revolver which was kept in the machine as protection against highwaymen, and shot her through the head. I believe she died almost immediately."[267] He concluded, "Then it dawned on me the horrible deed I had done, [and] I decided the best thing to do was to bring the body to the police station and surrender."[268]

New's mother, Mrs. Burger, confirmed that her son was the son of Senator New and that she and the senator "were married when we were mere children. I was only 16 at the time. A woman came between us when my boy was 4 years old, broke up our home, and we were divorced."[269]

Mrs. Burger said that her son had been infatuated with Frieda Lesser, the first serious relationship the young man had enjoyed. Gloating about his impeccable military record and his lack of any prior arrests, Mrs. Burger said that "he neither smokes, drinks, nor chews. He has no bad habits."[270]

Accompanying the dispatches from Los Angeles was a flash from Washington, D.C., indicating that Senator New denied that he and Mrs. Burger were ever married or divorced. "The only thing I care to add is that the statement from any sources that Mrs. Burger and I were ever either married or divorced at any time or under any name is absolutely untrue," Senator New said.[271]

By the next day, the headlines had grown worse. Not only did the Los Angeles Police Department report that young Harry New had tried to commit suicide inside his jail cell in the overnight hours, but more details about why he and Frieda Lesser had argued emerged as well. New told police detectives that the quarrel intensified when Lesser, who New believed was pregnant with his child, indicated that she planned to "have an operation which would make it impossible to the baby to be brought into life."[272] An autopsy on Lesser's body, however, revealed that she was not "in a delicate condition," as New apparently had believed.

Still talking to reporters, New and his mother, Mrs. Burger, continued to assert that he was the son of the junior senator from Indiana.

With little choice, on July 8, Senator New released a more detailed statement than his initial one and tried to cast the whole matter in the more positive light of personal responsibility: "I just have this to say about the whole deplorable matter. More than 30 years ago, when I was in my 20s and unmarried, I knew Mrs. Burger. There was never, at any time, a marriage between us. Conditions arose which I did not care to dispute which resulted in my doing everything in my power to make amends then and later."[273] He added, "Whatever I did in that direction was of my own accord and no one else had anything whatever to do with it. The affair was ended 30 years ago. Since that time, the people of my home city are the best judge of what my life has been. I never have shirked any responsibility that has come to me, and I never shall."[274]

Although failing to win a second term to the U.S. Senate, the elder New's longtime Republican friends came through for him, as President Warren G. Harding (1865–1923) appointed him U.S. postmaster general in 1923. Harding's successor, President Calvin Coolidge (1872–1933), retained New has head of the postal service from 1925 until the end of the Coolidge administration in 1933.

New retired to a home in Bethesda, Maryland, and spent summers at a cottage in Michigan but never again returned to Indiana until his death in May 1937. He is buried at Crown Hill Cemetery in Indianapolis.

MAKE ROOM IN THE JAIL FOR A MAYOR AND A GOVERNOR

The May 1925 Republican primaries gave the Ku Klux Klan an opportunity to demonstrate its domination of local and state elections in Indianapolis. Banker and real estate developer John L. Duvall (1874–1962), a former Marion County treasurer and Klan member, ran for mayor that year and defeated an anti-Klan candidate for the GOP nomination for mayor.[275]

Duvall was elected in November in an election marked by low voter turnout. Along with Duvall, six of nine council seats were won by pro-Klan Republicans in the fall election and resulted in neighborhood segregation policies passed in 1926. Later overturned by the courts, the law would have allowed white residents to legally keep blacks out of their neighborhoods.

This was a powerful period in Indianapolis for the Klan and those who shared their views on race. The *Fiery Cross*, the weekly national newspaper of the Klan, began publishing in Indianapolis in 1921 and eventually was taken over by the KKK's Indiana grand dragon, D.C. Stephenson (1891–1961).

In addition to backing Duvall and his council supporters, the paper also highlighted local clergy who offered sermons favorable to the Klan and pointed out those who did not. Names of prominent Catholic businessmen were also published, asking Klan members to boycott them. At its height, the paper's circulation rose to 100,000 and expanded to twelve pages.[276]

Despite the Klan support, just one year into office, Duvall's political empire began to crumble. His demise followed the arrest (and eventual conviction) of Stephenson in a Hamilton County court for the April 1925 rape and murder of a young statehouse clerk, Madge Oberholtzer (1896–1925).

Duvall's close association with Stephenson brought his 1925 campaign under heavy scrutiny, revealing that he had accepted cash payments from Klan insiders for political appointments. He was eventually convicted and served a thirty-day jail sentence and paid a $1,000 fine. His sentence may have been more severe had the judge known what secrets Stephenson held, but those didn't come out until after the trial.

Sensing that trouble was at hand, Duvall attempted to pull a fast one by appointing his wife, Maude, as the city controller, knowing that the controller succeeded the mayor should the mayor be removed from office. With his conviction, Duvall resigned his post, and his wife immediately became mayor. Her fifteen-minute term as mayor consisted of appointing Duvall's associate, Claude E. Negley, as city controller and then resigning herself. Negley's term as mayor lasted only from October 27 to November 9, until Democrats finally wrestled control of city hall away from the corrupt Duvall interests.

While Duvall's downfall played out, Stephenson continued to cool his heels in a prison cell, waiting for a pardon from Governor Edward L. Jackson (1873–1954) that would never come. Stephenson finally summoned the Marion County prosecutor to his jail cell and began spilling his guts. "There is a vacant chair next to mine in the [prison] jail factory," Stephenson was quoted as saying. "I am lonely and I am yearning for some of my playmates."[277]

Among his revelations, a signed pledge from Duvall read:

In return for the political support of D.C. Stephenson, in the event I am elected mayor of Indianapolis, Indiana, I promise not to appoint any person as a member of the board of public works without they first have the endorsement of D.C. Stephenson. I fully agree and promise to appoint Claude Worley as chief of police and Earl Klinck as a captain.[278]

As Mayor Duvall was suffering humiliation for his own graft and corruption, criminal charges would also soon overtake two other public officials on the other end of Market Street, most notably two Klan-made Indiana governors, Edward L. Jackson and his predecessor, Warren T. McCray (1865–1938).

As governor, McCray supported educational reforms in the state but, interestingly, declared before the legislature that Hoosiers wanted "a season of government economy and a period of legislative inaction and rest."[279]

McCray ended up angering his key Klan supporters after a private and public tussle with Jackson, then serving as the state's secretary of state, who wanted to grant an official state charter to the KKK. McCray asked the state's attorney general to revoke the charter granted by Jackson, which he refused to do.

Jackson's role as secretary of state and his unsavory interactions with Governor McCray in that role ultimately spelled his doom. But for now, Jackson was a Klan hero, and McCray had won the ire of Klan leaders. McCray's repudiation of the Klan reached its zenith when he refused to declare "Klan Day" at the Indiana State Fair that was to include a cross burning on the state fairgrounds in Indianapolis.

Behind the scenes, McCray was facing serious personal financial difficulties. His business interests had suffered from his time in public life, as well as from a farm depression affecting the Midwest in 1921. Desperate, McCray "resorted to fraud to obtain loans."[280]

The governor received a $155,000 loan from the State Agriculture Board—an obvious conflict of interest—and used the funds for personal expenses rather than for his cattle operation. He also wrote "a large number of fraudulent promissory notes, some of which he forged with the names of other people, [and] he attempted to sell these notes to banks that did business with the state as collateral for loans."[281]

While the banks cooperated out of fear of losing large state deposits, they did so grudgingly, and McCray's schemes came unraveled. In March 1924, a Marion County court tried the governor on a charge of embezzlement for the $155,000 loan from the state. The trial ended with a hung jury.

Federal prosecutors, however, were not done with McCray and indicted him on mail fraud charges related to his using the postal service to sell and distribute the fraudulent promissory notes. Convicted on the federal charges, McCray resigned as governor on April 30, 1924, and the unassuming Lieutenant Governor Emmett F. Branch (1874–1932) of Martinsville became governor.

McCray was sent to a federal penitentiary in Atlanta, Georgia, for a ten-year sentence. In 1930, President Herbert Hoover (1874–1964), a fellow Republican, granted him a full pardon. Back in Indiana, McCray rebuilt his business but died suddenly in 1938.

McCray's one-time friend turned political enemy Jackson took advantage of the situation (and a lack of political support for newly installed Governor Branch) to wage his own bid for governor in the 1924 election. A former judge and county prosecutor from Howard County, Jackson quickly distinguished himself among Indianapolis pols, particularly for his open and fierce devotion to the powerful Klan.

"For his part, Jackson saw the Klan as an immensely popular, bipartisan group that had repackaged a message of morality, Americanism, Protestantism, and Prohibition, lifted wholesale from the state's churches and patriotic organizations," historian Jason Lantzer wrote.[282]

Although deeply aligned with the Klan, Jackson went out of his way to tell Catholic, Jewish and black voters that they had nothing to fear. Further, Jackson wrapped himself in the flag of prohibition and successfully and inaccurately cast his Democratic opponents as "wet" on the issue of legalized drinking.

One year into office, however, Jackson's personal and political struggles mounted. As shameful and ultimately criminal charges against Stephenson spelled the ruin of his political empire, Jackson did nothing to help, ignoring suggestions that he offer Stephenson a pardon. Stephenson's anger grew as he festered in an Indiana State Prison cell on a charge of murder.

Stephenson would get the last laugh. Among the documents he turned over to prosecutors were ones indicating that Jackson, as secretary of state, had carried a Klan-sponsored $10,000 bribe to Governor McCray in order to influence the appointment of the Marion County prosecutor in Indianapolis. Governor McCray had not accepted the bribe, but Jackson *had* offered it, the documents proved.[283]

Jackson was eventually tried on charges of official misconduct but never faced a conviction or jail time because the state's statute of limitations on the bribe to Governor McCray had expired. Jackson refused to resign as governor, despite the scandal, and finished his term in January 1929.

A political outcast, Jackson failed in his effort to start a law practice in Indianapolis after he left office. After suffering a stroke in 1948, he lay bedridden in a farmhouse in Orange County in southern Indiana before he died in 1954.

JESSE L. DICKINSON OVERCOMES JIM CROW

Jesse L. Dickinson (1906–1982) was not Indiana's first African American legislator, but he was one who fought vigorously to change the remnants of Jim Crow laws that still hung over the state and Indianapolis.

First elected to the Indiana House of Representatives in 1942 on the Democratic ticket, Dickinson came to Indianapolis from South Bend for the 1943 session and was astonished by what he found in terms of where he could eat and where he could sleep at night during sessions.

Indiana historian Justin E. Walsh noted that "black legislators during the first three decades of the era [1930–70] selected lesser facilities [for housing] because they had no choice. Blacks in Indianapolis were not welcome at any downtown hotel or private club, and could not dine at any downtown Indianapolis restaurants before the mid-1950s."[284]

Initially, Dickinson took his "meals" on session days by eating what he could purchase at a snack bar in the basement of the statehouse. Otherwise, he had to walk six blocks west of the capitol to a black neighborhood along Indiana Avenue where cafés were operated by blacks.

Dickinson was also excluded during his earliest terms in the House from attending legislative breakfasts and dinners because they were held at the infamous Claypool Hotel in downtown Indianapolis—a hotel that didn't serve blacks until 1955.

Walsh reported that Dickinson's struggles for lodging were even more troubling, having to rent a private room in a boardinghouse after finding the segregated Indianapolis YMCA for blacks unsuitable. Dickinson also told of struggles that continued beyond Indianapolis, including an experience he had while riding home from Indianapolis in a car driven by State Senator D. Russell Bontrager, an Elkhart Republican.

"A restaurant in Rochester refused to serve Dickinson," Walsh wrote. "Bontrager demanded to see the owner and informed him that Dickinson was a member of the Indiana General Assembly. The owner replied, 'I don't care if he is the President of the United States, he will not be served.'"[285]

From then on, when explaining why he was voting "no" on a particular bill, Dickinson would often quote, "I don't care if the sponsor of the bill is the President of the United States, I'm still voting no."[286]

As early as 1953, Dickinson was fighting to end Indiana's sad connections to Jim Crow. "I help pay taxes for Indiana's state parks, but I have never been in one, because I know if I went there, I would be humiliated," he said as he urged legislators to pass a bill banning discrimination in state-owned public accommodations.[287]

After being elevated by the voters to the Indiana State Senate in 1959, Dickinson joined Senator Robert L. Brokenburr, an Indianapolis Republican and African American elected to the Senate in 1941, in sponsoring landmark bills to guarantee equal accommodations for persons in cafés, hotels, hospitals, public housing and amusement facilities regardless of race. As *Jet* magazine reported at the time:

> *An Indiana state senator, who once ate cheese and crackers because restaurants denied him service, said he is confident the state legislature "has the courage" to pass a bill ending all Jim Crow practices. Sen. Jesse Dickinson (D-South Bend) made the statement after he and Sen. Robert Brokenburr (R-Indianapolis), the only other Negro state senator, introduced a bill to put "teeth" in an 1885 Indiana law which prohibits discrimination.*[288]

Dickinson retired from the legislature in 1961 after six terms in the House and one term in the Senate and served many years as an executive with the South Bend Public Housing Authority. The Jesse L. Dickinson Middle School was dedicated there in 1976.

Dickinson's son, Valjean L. Dickinson, was elected to one term in the Indiana House from 1964 to 1966. Later, Dickinson's daughter-in-law (and Valjean's wife), Mae Dickinson, won multiple terms in the House from Indianapolis between 1990 and 2008.

GEORGE WALLACE'S NORTHERN ENCROACHMENT

Indiana Democrats, and Hoosiers in general, are sometimes embarrassed to admit that the derisive name given to the state ("the Mississippi of the Midwest") sometimes is all too accurate.

That likely is how a lot of Democrats in the 1960s and 1970s felt as Alabama governor George C. Wallace (1919–1998)—a kingpin of the once powerful segregationist movement in America—continued to attract a lot of votes in Indiana.

For Wallace, Indiana votes were a major coup. To do so well in a state so far out of the Deep South gave Wallace and his supporters ammunition that he was a serious contender for the presidency and that he was not just a second-tier regional candidate.

Wallace first made headlines in 1964 by vowing to challenge the presumptive Democratic nominee, President Lyndon B. Johnson (1908–1973), who had ascended to the presidency in November 1963 following the assassination of President John F. Kennedy (1917–1963).

Wallace, likely speaking for many southern Democrats, loathed Johnson as a "Texas sell-out" for his positions on the 1964 Civil Rights Act. Wallace had already staged his famous yet unsuccessful "stand in the doorway" against integration by trying to block the admission of African American students to the University of Alabama—and he wasn't done riding the circuit. Wallace dubbed it his own campaign against "civil wrongs" and warned that Johnson's support of the Civil Rights Act would "destroy every neighborhood school in the country."[289]

As he entered the May 1964 Democratic presidential primary in Indiana, Wallace may have calculated that his chances were better than elsewhere as Indiana governor Matt Welsh (1912–1995) was standing in as a "favorite son" nominee for Johnson. It was a tactic that the Johnson campaign used in several states so the president could remain above the fray.

Alabama governor George C. Wallace, circa 1968. *Library of Congress LC-U9-18605-18A.*

Wallace made a big splash as his plane landed at Weir Cook International Airport in Indianapolis, complete with its "Stand Up for America" signs and Confederate flag symbols. Wallace told Indianapolis reporters that he was running in Indiana "because I want to let the people here have an effective way of opposing some of the trends going on in Washington. I have the highest regard for Governor Welsh. He is a fine man."[290]

The feeling was not mutual. Welsh, known for living by his personal motto that "It doesn't cost you anything to be a gentleman," shed some of that persona in taking on his fellow Democratic governor from Alabama, who he said was "trying to wreck the Democratic Party."[291]

Welsh said that Wallace's campaign "smells sweet, but it has the taste of death." Welsh reminded his fellow Hoosier Democrats that Wallace

> is the man who tolerated the presence of billboards in his state before the assassination [of President Kennedy] which demanded: "Kayo the Kennedys." This is the man whose beliefs were responsible for the deaths of innocent children in the bombing of a Sunday school class. This is the man who stood by while dogs were set upon human beings and fire hoses were turned on groups of peaceful demonstrators. This is the man who even today is actively denying Negro children access to the University of Alabama. This is the man who is trying to destroy the political system in the United States as we know it, and who seeks to discredit President Lyndon B. Johnson. This is the man who flies the Confederate flag over the Statehouse in Alabama in place of the Stars and Stripes.[292]

At an appearance at Butler University in Indianapolis, Wallace attempted to reassure students and faculty that "I'm not a racist. I'm against interracial marriages. I think the Negro race ought to stay pure and the white race stay pure. God intended for white people to stay white, Chinese to stay yellow, and Negroes to stay black. All mankind is the handiwork of God."[293]

In the end, Welsh easily dispatched Wallace by a vote of 368,401 to 170,146. But Wallace's strong showing stole the headlines and gave his campaign steam as he went on to later primaries.

Wallace ran again in 1968, but this time under the banner of the American Independent Party. In November, his "southern strategy" polled 9 percent of the vote in Indiana (and 13.5 percent nationally) against former vice president

Richard M. Nixon (1913–1996) and the sitting vice president, Hubert H. Humphrey (1911–1978), essentially keeping Humphrey from the White House.

By 1972, Wallace was back in the Democratic fold in a race that no one expected the Democrats to win against Nixon, the popular incumbent Republican. Wallace's entry into the Indiana Democratic primary again caused great anxiety among Democratic leaders.

Time magazine described Wallace's Indiana effort as "characteristically helter-skelter" and made heavy notice of a twenty-five-dollar-per-plate Wallace luncheon at the Indianapolis Hilton "that drew, among others, Grand Dragon William Chaney of the state Ku Klux Klan, and Frank Thompson, head of the local John Birch Society chapter."[294]

If given more time, Wallace may have won the Indiana primary. As is, Humphrey carried the day with 47 percent of the vote, barely besting Wallace back at 42 percent. His favorable Indiana showing matched earlier solid performances in the Wisconsin and Florida primaries.

"Wallace was helped by a heavy Republican crossover vote," *Time* magazine analyzed. "Humphrey had a 38,000-vote margin in the popular vote, with most of his edge coming from Indianapolis and Gary, which have the state's heaviest concentrations of blacks."[295]

Just days after the Indiana primary, Wallace moved on to Maryland and Michigan for their primary contests. At a May 15, 1972 shopping center parking lot rally in Laurel, Maryland, Wallace's life would change forever. A gunman, Arthur Bremer, stepped from the crowd and shot Wallace five times. Three others were seriously wounded. From that moment on, the outspoken Alabama governor would be confined to a wheelchair, and his presidential ambitions would be ended forever.

A HOOSIER NOT TO BE CONFUSED WITH THE FACTS

Indiana's Earl F. Landgrebe (1916–1986) never made much of a name for himself during his three terms in Congress, terms highlighted by his loyal and staunch defense of President Richard M. Nixon even as everyone else was abandoning "Tricky Dicky."

Landgrebe's now-famous quote is more well known than he is. In the midst of House hearings considering Articles of Impeachment brought forth against Nixon in August 1974, Indiana's Landgrebe stood firm. He said that Nixon had done "no treasonable offense" in his view.[296]

He famously added, "Don't confuse me with the facts, I have a closed mind. I'm going to stick with my President even if he and I have to be taken out of this building and shot."[297]

His quote came just as Nixon had doomed himself, with White House documents clearly showing that the administration had actively worked to thwart the FBI's investigation of the Watergate break-in. Landgrebe was in a select group of forty-two members of Congress still supporting the president that was summoned to the White House to hear Nixon declare his plans to give up the fight. Nixon became the first U.S. president to resign on August 9, 1974.

It wasn't the first time Landgrebe had made headlines. While serving as a member of the Indiana General Assembly, Landgrebe was known for his staunch Lutheran views and the practice of handing out evangelical religious "tracts" to anyone nearby. "The practice got him into trouble when he visited the Soviet Union in 1972," reports Indiana historian Justin E. Walsh. "Landgrebe was seized by Russian police and interrogated after placing copies of the Gospel according to St. Matthew on the counter in a Moscow department store." He was later released.[298]

Landgrebe was forced to retire from public life by voters in the 1974 Democratic landslide, and he told reporters in 1979, "I struggled with Nixon [on the Watergate issue] for a year. I studied. I delved into it. I searched my soul."[299]

THE BUTZ OF A BAD JOKE

The life story of Earl L. Butz (1909–2008) is a typical American story: young man grows up on the farm and leaves to become a powerful and noteworthy public official. People in Indiana had long been proud of Butz, a farm boy with an agricultural degree from Purdue University, and of his tenure as secretary of agriculture for Presidents Nixon and Gerald R. Ford (1913–2006).

It was Butz's unceremonious departure from public life, however, that tends to be what most people remember about him. Ford fired Butz—or

Butz resigned, depending on who you asked—after *Rolling Stone* magazine ran a story containing a racist and vulgar "joke" that Butz had told to famed crooner and conservative activist Pat Boone and Watergate figure James Dean.

Butz made a bad move. Dean was working on assignment as a correspondent for *Rolling Stone* in its coverage of the 1976 presidential election and would later report that the "joke" was offered in reply to a question from Boone aboard an airplane flight about why the Republicans—the party of Lincoln—struggled so much to attract black voters. *Time* magazine attempted to retell Butz's remarks, carried in Dean's story, in a sanitized version by noting that

> *Butz started by telling a dirty joke involving intercourse between a dog and a skunk. He was quoted as adding, "I'll tell you what the coloreds want. It's three things: first, a tight pussy; second, loose shoes; and third, a warm place to shit." After some indecision, Dean used the line in* Rolling Stone, *attributing it to an unnamed* [Ford] *Cabinet officer. But* New Times *magazine enterprisingly sleuthed out Butz's identity by checking the itineraries of all Cabinet members.*[300]

Beyond the fact that Butz's comments were so blue that they couldn't be repeated in most settings, it wasn't his first fall-out on the public stage. His feigned Italian accent while visiting the Vatican in Rome had won him rebuke previously. "Let's be honest, I'm controversial," he said at the time. "I don't hesitate to speak my mind."[301]

Butz retired from public life following the scandal but gained headlines again briefly in 1981 after pleading guilty to federal tax evasion charges for failing to report income on his 1978 tax return. He served thirty days of a five-year prison term, was fined $10,000 and was ordered to pay $61,183 in civil penalties.[302]

Butz eventually returned to Purdue University and Indiana as a well-regarded expert in agriculture. He died at ninety-eight in 2010, earning the distinction of having the longest lifespan of any presidential cabinet member in U.S. history.

NEGLEY'S NEGLIGENCE

On April 10, 1985, Indiana's elected state superintendent of public instruction, Dr. Harold H. Negley (1921–2008), resigned his office, bringing to a climax a long and ugly investigation that revealed a level of graft and corruption unknown at the Indiana Statehouse in decades.

Negley offered his resignation to Governor Robert D. Orr (1917–2004), a fellow Republican, by saying, "My personal difficulties have overshadowed the critical educational issues which face us today. I therefore, regretfully, resign the office of state superintendent of public instruction, effective immediately."[303]

A native of Indianapolis, Negley first won statewide office in 1972 and was completing his fourth term as the state's top educator when a criminal indictment finally brought him down. A former schoolteacher, principal and social studies textbook author, it was a disgraceful end for a proud man.

Governor Orr said, "I regret this whole episode has taken place. It has had a searing effect on the Department of Education and certainly on Dr. Negley's family."[304]

Marion County's up-and-coming prosecutor, Steve Goldsmith (later elected mayor of Indianapolis), said that "there is no plea bargain" for Negley in exchange for his resignation from office but that Negley had engaged in discussions about testifying before the Marion County Grand Jury.

The grand jury probe had been widespread—more than three hundred Department of Education employees received questionnaires about their activities, or those they witnessed, as state employees. The employees and investigators would eventually unearth the truth: nonexistent or "ghost employees" on the state payroll, as well as forced political contributions from employees for Negley's campaigns and personal expenses.[305]

The investigation primarily centered on Negley and two of his top aides, Parker B. Eaton and Raymond A. Slaby. Eaton was indicted by the grand jury on an obstruction of justice charge in March 1985 for allegedly threatening to shred incriminating documents. It was later revealed that Eaton's "doctoral degree" in education was awarded based on work at two defunct, nonaccredited "colleges" in Florida and Texas.[306]

Indianapolis Star bird-dog reporter Joe Gelarden uncovered that Eaton had a prior criminal record for shoplifting a bottle of whiskey from a store, while

Slaby had pleaded guilty and received a suspended sentence in 1982 for an official misconduct charge from a previous stint in local government.

Gelarden also wrote that "[e]ducation department workers say Eaton was the chief collector for Negley's political and personal fund drives… [and] the grand jury has been told that education department workers holding clerical and executive positions say Eaton's collection methods implied, in less than subtle ways, that their jobs depended on their political and personal donations."[307]

A day later, Eaton confirmed to Gelarden that he had personally collected more than $174,000 in contributions from state employees between 1980 and 1983. "I can't see how anyone said I pressured anyone," Eaton said. "Not one person was ever dismissed because they did not contribute."[308]

Negley's resignation did not save him from a grand jury indictment for ghost employment and official misconduct on April 19, 1985. Salby, Eaton and three others were also charged.[309]

In June 1985, Negley pleaded guilty to two felony charges of ghost employment and one misdemeanor charge of official misconduct. He was given a one-year suspended sentence, fined $1,000 and ordered to perform two hundred hours of community service.[310]

DAN QUAYLE'S "EXCELLENT ADVENTURE"

When news broke during the August 1988 Republican National Convention in New Orleans, Louisiana, that GOP nominee George H.W. Bush had selected a U.S. senator from Indiana to be his running mate, everyone immediately assumed that Bush meant the senior senator from Indiana, Richard G. Lugar.

To almost everyone's surprise, Bush had actually selected the *junior* senator from Indiana, J. Danforth Quayle, who was completing just his second term in the U.S. Senate. Elected in an upset of Democrat Birch Bayh in the Republican landslide of 1980, Quayle had a short list of legislative accomplishments and an even shorter list of people outside Indiana who knew his name.

It didn't matter. Bush had taken his own counsel and went with a "surprise" pick and someone younger than himself in order to help step out from the shadow of term-limited president Ronald Reagan (1911–2004). Quayle likely reminded Bush of his own son, George W. Bush—both were of the same generation (born within seventeen months of each other in the postwar baby boom years of 1946–47), and both had avoided military service in Vietnam via the National Guard.

The media—as it's apt to do—went looking for information about this seemingly unknown senator from Indiana. As that happened, the Bush team went into damage control as problems quickly arose, not only surrounding the résumé of Quayle and his preparation to be "one heartbeat away from the Presidency" but also his lack of active military service in the Vietnam War. (Quayle, son and grandson of powerful Indiana newspaper publishers, had secured a stateside assignment writing news releases for the Indiana National Guard.)

As the Bush-Quayle campaign kicked off from the steps of the Huntington County Courthouse in Huntington, Indiana, on August 20, 1988, it was clear from the start that it was going to be a bumpy ride with Dan Quayle in the passenger's seat.

Although thousands of loyal Hoosiers showed up to cheer the GOP standard-bearers, dozens of reporters from around the nation and the world had also descended on Huntington. As the Bush-Quayle team tried to move onward and upward from questions about Quayle's background, the campaign began to seal Quayle off from the media. Left with no alternative, the reporters shouted their questions to Bush and Quayle at the end of the Huntington rally.

Reporter Maureen Dowd described the scene for readers of the *New York Times* as follows:

> *Mr. Quayle was quickly hooked up to a public address system on the edge of the crowd. His hometown boosters were thus able to hear his exchange with the press and express their partisan feelings. This created a surly scene. Starting with the first question, about whether he had used influence to get into the National Guard, the crowd drowned out reporters' questions with boos and shouts of "Quayle!, Quayle!," "boring" and "what branch of the service were you in?" Boos continued as the candidate was asked if he regretted not serving in Vietnam...and exactly what he did in the National Guard besides working in public relations ("I also served in the*

kitchen patrol and I peeled a lot of potatoes," he replied). The press, in turn, became combative and persisted with sharp questions. When Ellen Hume of The Wall Street Journal *asked Mr. Quayle how he felt when "people were dying in Vietnam while you were writing press releases," the crowd began making personal comments about the reporter, calling for "the redhead" to leave him alone.*[311]

Quayle's assertions aside, the questions did not subside. Democrats and the media continued to pound Quayle about his background—and Bush about his judgment in offering the VP position to the young senator. Bush continued to state his support for Quayle remaining on the ticket despite immense public and private pressure to dump him.

Bush-Quayle won the 1988 election, despite an embarrassing and memorable vice presidential debate performance by Quayle that produced one of greatest political "zingers" in history. As Quayle repeatedly compared his record and experience to that of President John Kennedy, Democratic vice presidential nominee Lloyd Bentsen (1921–2006) could stand no more, turned to Quayle and said, "Senator, I served with Jack Kennedy, I knew Jack Kennedy, Jack Kennedy was a friend of mine. Senator, you're no Jack Kennedy." The audience roared, and all Quayle could manage was, "That was really uncalled for, Senator."[312]

As vice president, Quayle's problems persisted, with the media giving him no pale. Quayle didn't help matters, correcting a young student with the wrong spelling of the word "potato" during a scripted elementary school visit. His twisted tongue in remembering quotes also served to trip him up. For those who knew Quayle from his days in Indiana, they could hardly recognize the caricature that was being created.

Reporters continued to poke around into Quayle's background, raising questions about his admission to the Indiana University School of Law in Indianapolis on a seat normally reserved for a minority student (and despite a reportedly average performance as an undergraduate at DePauw University) and about his past ties to a lobbyist turned *Playboy* model, Paula Parkinson.

Still lingering today are rumors that as a young law student Quayle purchased marijuana from a man named Brett C. Kimberlin—a convicted felon who became known as "the Speedway bomber." From his federal jail cell, Kimberlin continued to raise the specter of having sold Quayle marijuana in the parking lot of an Indianapolis Burger Chef restaurant. Kimberlin even suggested that Quayle's influence as vice president had prolonged his stay in federal prison—and in solitary confinement.[313]

The Dukakis-Bentsen ticket of 1988 was not above trying to find out more. One-time Democratic strategist (and now *ABC News* personality) George Stephanopolous wrote in his 1999 book *All Too Human* about his quick trip to Indianapolis to verify the story:

> *In the fall of 1988, when the Dukakis campaign was going down the tubes, I was part of a "rapid response" team doing a remarkably ineffectual job of rebutting Republican attacks. But late in the race, a federal prisoner named Brett Kimberlin was telling reporters he once sold drugs to Dan Quayle, and that Quayle might have sold some himself. A rumor reached me that years earlier, a grand jury examining the evidence had covered it up under pressure from prosecutors close to Quayle's family. If I could find the disgruntled grand jurors and convince them to talk, we'd win—and I'd be a hero. So I bought a plane ticket to Indianapolis and holed up in the airport Holiday Inn with photocopied courthouse records. After a day of cold-calling people who had no idea what I was talking about, I knew I was on a fool's errand. My sleuthing wasn't illegal, just criminally incompetent and a little slimy.[314]*

Quayle refused interviews on the subject, with Bush's White House press secretary David Beckwith declaring, "The Vice President has never used marijuana, or, to his knowledge, met Brett Kimberlin."[315]

In his 1994 memoir *Standing Firm*, Quayle described his irritation at the attention the media afforded to Kimberlin's allegations just weeks before the critical 1988 presidential election:

> *[T]he press felt there had to be some drug story about the first [baby] boomer candidate, and in the last weeks of the campaign a convicted felon bent on exploiting the system cooked up just the story some of them wanted. Brett Kimberlin was a perjurer doing a 51 year federal prison sentence for terrorizing the town of Speedway, Indiana, by planting eight bombs in seven days…He said he wanted to show how "hypocritical" my anti drug positions were. There was not a shred of truth to his bizarre accusation,*

nor a single witness to back it up, and if anyone could have less credibility I have a hard time imagining who it would be…But the media in the frantic final days of the campaign didn't care about facts and ran with the story anyway…Kimberlin's story was so ridiculous that it should never have made its way into the mainstream media.[316]

Bush-Quayle were finished in January 1993, defeated for a second term by a young governor from Arkansas (Bill Clinton) who, like Quayle, had also avoided military service in Vietnam. Clinton's young running mate, a senator from Tennessee (Al Gore), had served tours of duty in Vietnam. Quayle's 2000 campaign for the Republican presidential nomination ended quickly after disappointing finishes in early GOP primaries.

A SCANDAL WORTH BETTING ON

In 1988, Indiana voters overwhelmingly broke one of the state's last barriers to legalized gambling by approving the creation of a statewide lottery. Forthwith, the Hoosier Lottery began selling scratch-off tickets in October 1989 to the strains of the Pointer Sisters (appearing in person in Indianapolis) singing their hit, "I'm So Excited!"

The arrival of the Hoosier Lottery was a big event in Indiana politics. Before the voters' approval, gambling of any sort had long been banned in Indiana. That's all changed, of course, as Indiana now has not only a lottery but also several casinos and pari-mutuel wagering on horse races running constantly.

For the state's new young governor, Evan Bayh, elected at the age of thirty-three in a rare political shift in Indiana from the Republicans to the Democrats—setting up the lottery was high stakes business. And Bayh promised an aboveboard approach that stressed integrity and even fashioned his appointment of the state's first lottery director as one of his most important.

Bayh picked Lake County prosecutor Jack Crawford for the $80,000-per-year post, a position then paying almost as much as the governor made. Crawford was known as a skilled prosecutor who had led many complicated and controversial criminal cases in Lake County (the northwest Indiana county lying in the shadow of Chicago). For Crawford, it was a move meant to further his ambition for statewide office—in fact, to one day succeed Bayh and become governor of Indiana.[317]

It didn't take long for the Hoosier Lottery to start producing winners— including an Indianapolis woman who earned the distinction of being the first $1 million winner in early December 1989 on the lottery's wildly popular weekly TV show, *Hoosier Millionaire*.

That news, however, was quickly overshadowed by revelations that Crawford had abruptly resigned as head of the Hoosier Lottery, and the Bayh administration went into damage control mode. Listing only "personal reasons," Crawford said that he resigned in a letter given to the governor on Sunday afternoon, December 10, 1989.

The governor was offering few additional details, saying only that "Mr. Crawford's reasons for resigning were personal, not governmental. Therefore, they should be discussed by the individuals involved, not by a politician at a press conference."[318] Bayh added, "I think my role as governor is to ensure the integrity of government, to ensure that the lottery is being well run. I will not engage in a public discussion of a personal, private matter."[319]

Reporters could smell blood in the water and quickly surrounded Crawford for more details. In a surreal impromptu news conference carried live on local television from Crawford's unfurnished Indianapolis apartment, he sat on the floor and openly confessed that he had engaged in an extramarital affair with a subordinate and that he had resigned from his post under "mutual agreement" with the governor.

Crawford said that his relationship with one of his employees was based on love—not sexual harassment—saying that it was "simply a case of a love affair that went very bad. It's nothing more than that. It's not a case of violence, threats, beatings, intimidations, coercions or efforts on my part to harass anyone."[320]

Crawford's world had begun to crumble without his knowledge a few days earlier when his love interest, Mary L. Cartwright, privately approached a top aide to Governor Bayh and alleged that she felt pressured to keep the sexual liaison with Crawford going in order to keep her job. Interestingly, during his short tenure as head of the lottery, Crawford had authorized only one raise for an employee: a $3,000 boost for Cartwright.

Cartwright, eight years older than Crawford, had relocated from Lake County to Indianapolis at Crawford's invitation. In Lake County, she had been a top aide in the prosecutor's office. For the lottery, Crawford had tapped her to be his director of personnel. No one knew—including the governor or Crawford's shocked wife—that Cartwright had been Crawford's lover for many of the thirteen years they worked together in Lake County and in Indianapolis.

"I loved Mary Cartwright, clearly, but I didn't love her well," Crawford told reporters through sobs and tears. "I have no one to blame for what's happened but myself. I have done some incredibly dumb things over the past several years."[321]

Crawford said that his wife and two sons had fled Indianapolis to return to Lake County—the marriage would eventually end. With the cat out of the bag by Crawford's own tearful admissions, Governor Bayh finally commented, calling Crawford's actions "deplorable."[322] "It seems to me entirely inappropriate for an important supervisor or a department head or someone in a position of trust to have a sexual relationship with an employee," the governor said.

Bayh said that had he known about the ongoing affair, he never would have hired Crawford. "Mr. Crawford was looked squarely in the eye by my chief of staff and asked, 'is there anything in your background that would be potentially embarrassing to you or this administration?' The answer was no," Bayh said.[323]

There was plenty of embarrassment to go around. Local newspapers and TV stations ran verbatim accounts of "love letters" Crawford had written to Cartwright that she had turned over to the Governor's Office. In the weeks that followed, Cartwright was terminated from her job at the Hoosier Lottery for reasons that state officials said were unrelated to the scandal.

Nothing of the scandal, however, seemed to affect the love that Indiana residents were quickly developing for the Hoosier Lottery. State Lottery Commission officials revealed that in its first month of operation, the lottery had produced $42.3 million in revenue for state coffers.[324]

No criminal charges were ever brought, and Crawford began to rebuild his life, opening a successful criminal defense law practice in Indianapolis in early 1990. It seemed that a lot of folks facing criminal charges liked the idea of having a former county prosecutor on their side of the case.

Crawford, still credited with getting Indiana's state lottery off the ground, years later offered interesting advice to his fellow Hoosiers about playing the lottery: "I helped create and design it, so I know that only the state government is making millions. Never play the lottery."[325]

A FOOTNOTE IN INDIANA POLITICS: DWAYNE M. BROWN

In most elections, the statewide post of clerk of the state supreme and appellate courts is not one that gathers headlines. In fact, the position was one eventually removed from the ballot altogether and is now appointed by the court. However, in 1990, the newly elected clerk of the courts, Dwayne M. Brown, made history.

Brown, a graduate of the Columbia University School of Law, became the state's first African American elected to statewide office. Two years later, in 1992, Pamela Carter repeated Brown's accomplishment when she was elected Indiana attorney general (a post Brown wanted for himself).

Brown and Carter generated a lot of high hopes and expectations, not only among African Americans in Indiana but also among Democrats, who began to see their fortunes change in 1988 after Governor Evan Bayh broke a two-decade hold on the state's top office by Republicans. Ambition for higher and bigger things, however, seemed to get in Brown's way from the start.

Admitted to the Indiana Bar in 1987, he quickly gained notice among Indianapolis lawyers and, just three years into his legal career, was elected to statewide office. But just a year or so into office, he wanted a higher office—either the attorney general's office or a seat in Congress (a seat already held by U.S. Representative Andy Jacobs Jr., an Indianapolis Democrat). His plans would be derailed after several young female staff members eventually came forward and reported Brown's political activities on state time and troubling, inappropriate personal behavior.

In all, six former female staff members in Brown's statehouse office made a slew of damaging allegations under oath that Brown had touched and kissed them and made suggestive remarks about their sex lives but most frequently commented about their feet and toes, offering gushing (and sometimes embarrassing) compliments about how nice their shoes or feet looked. The compliments went even further, with two women alleging that Brown asked to lick and suck their feet and toes.[326]

Brown's problems, however, extended beyond his inability to maintain proper boundaries with female staffers. He also, allegedly, regularly used state employees to advance his own personal political career. Three former female staffers said that Brown routinely asked them to perform political functions as a regular part of their jobs as state employees.

One staffer, Kolene Allen, also added another twist: Brown had invited her, on state time, to attend a daytime showing of the film *The Pelican Brief*, starring Julia Roberts and Denzel Washington (a film that features an interracial romantic interest between the two). Allen would later allege that during the film, Brown (who is black) made sexual advances on Allen (who is white).

"I asked him if it was strictly business, and he said it was," Allen testified during Brown's 1995 criminal trial on charges of ghost employment and official misconduct. "He said this movie would help me gain insight and educate me about politics."[327] Within days of attending the film, Allen said that Brown informed her she was receiving a Christmas bonus and increased her salary by $2,500.

"After he bumped my bonus up...I was flabbergasted. I had just been working there a week. I told him I felt bad he had given me the money, that I didn't deserve it," she said.[328] She told jurors in Brown's trial that he said, "Since I'm helping you, you can help me out by buying tickets for a fundraiser."[329]

In January 1994, just a month into her new job, Allen said that she received another $3,000 "bonus" after Brown quizzed her about her desire to buy a new car. She said that Brown told her that "he wanted to be more than a boss to his employees. He wants to be their friend and help them out, as they help him out."[330]

Allen later brought a civil sexual harassment suit against Brown and the state, claiming that Brown had "an obsession with her feet," repeatedly asking her if he could fondle and kiss her feet and making other sexual advances.[331]

In her civil suit, Allen said, "Brown asked that [she] remove her shoe in order that he could see her foot. He stated to [her] that he had a foot fetish," and she later learned she was hired because he was attracted to her feet.[332]

Three other women eventually alleged Brown had made similar advances to them—including comments about their feet—but the state's Equal Employment Opportunity Commission said that the claims had come in after deadlines imposed by federal law for making such claims.[333]

Brown defended himself in a sensational Indianapolis trial on seven counts of ghost employment and official misconduct. He denied on the stand in a calm voice all of the claims made against him by former female staff members. Although not a part of the criminal trial, regarding the allegations that he sexually harassed female employees regarding their feet and toes, Brown told reporters outside the court, "I would never do anything that would appear to be inappropriate behavior."[334] Brown acknowledged that the governmental and political functions of his office often became "intertwined" but denied using state employees to advance his own political ambitions.

On November 3, 1995, jurors convicted Brown on seven separate counts. At age thirty-three, his legal and political career lay in pieces on the ground.

During his December 1995 sentencing hearing, more than thirty letters of support were submitted asking for a light sentence for Brown, including ones from state legislators and prominent local attorneys. One of the letters from Brown's wife claimed that he had been victimized by "the politics of defamation."[335]

At his sentencing hearing, Brown read a prepared statement, saying, "I have suffered embarrassment and public humiliation and apologize to my family for the hurt and pain they have suffered during this ordeal, and to anyone else who has suffered as a result of my conviction."[336] He predicted he could continue to make "a positive contribution to society" and asked for "a just and appropriate sentence."[337]

In the end, Marion Superior Court judge Gary L. Miller said that Brown had twisted the principle of public service to mean "that government was of Dwayne Brown, by Dwayne Brown, and for Dwayne Brown." The judge added, "You are a thief, Mr. Brown. You've stolen the public trust. You've stolen the hopes and dreams of your family members and friends and destroyed a very promising political and legal career."[338]

Miller then sentenced Brown to a suspended sentence of three years, with two years of probation required. He also ordered Brown to pay fines and costs of about $10,000 and to perform 240 hours of community service.[339]

Brown's troubles were not over. The Disciplinary Commission recommended suspending Brown's license to practice law in Indiana for five years. He also lost the appeal of his criminal conviction, to go along with his loss in the May 1994 Democratic primary in a challenge to Congressman Jacobs.

DAN BURTON'S GLASS HOUSE SHATTERS

Congressman Dan Burton of Indianapolis—who represented one of the nation's "most Republican" Congressional districts, stretching north into Carmel and all of Hamilton County—quickly gained power with the historic 1994 GOP takeover of the U.S. House of Representatives.

Born in Indianapolis in 1938, "Danny" Burton overcame many obstacles in his life, most notably what he has often disclosed as a violent childhood at the hand of his alcoholic father.

In 1950, when Burton was just twelve years old, he and his brother (Indiana State Representative Woody Burton, R-Greenwood) and their sister were sent to the Marion County Children's Guardian Home after their father abducted and beat their mother.[340]

The parallels between Burton's young life and that of President Bill Clinton are startling. Clinton has written and spoken of his early life in Arkansas with an abusive and alcoholic stepfather who would batter his mother. And while both Burton and Clinton became highly accomplished and brilliantly able politicians, both were derailed (at least temporarily) by their own shared personal problems.

Early in 1998, as political scandal engulfed the Clinton administration and the president eventually admitted to an extramarital affair with a White House intern, it was Burton who told writers at the *Indianapolis Star* that the president was "a scumbag."[341] "If I could prove 10 percent of what I believe happened, he'd [Clinton] be gone. This guy's a scumbag. That's why I'm after him," Burton said.[342]

It was just the latest in a career filled with moralizing statements about the peccadilloes of other politicians—and Clinton, in particular, a favorite target of Burton both in the press and through his role as chair of the House Government Reform and Oversight Committee.

Burton's assessment of Clinton was also the kind of red meat that many of his staunchly conservative supporters loved to hear from their congressman. Outside his district, a *Chicago Tribune* editorial surmised that "Dan Burton is a crude, crass man who is a disgrace to his district, his state, his party and the House."[343]

Behind the scenes, all of the straight talk from the congressman only fueled a widespread and ultimately successful investigation by journalists and

Burton's political foes that revealed that Burton had not always conducted his own life to the same standard he seemingly held the president.

In September 1998, purportedly to stave off an upcoming exposé from the writers of *Vanity Fair* magazine, Burton disclosed to the *Indianapolis Star* that he himself had engaged an extramarital affair in the 1980s that had resulted in the birth of a child, a teenage boy at the time of the disclosure.

Burton acknowledged that he and his wife had been separated at times in the past and that he had "dated" outside their thirty-eight-year marriage. In his official statement, he said that he felt victimized by the Clinton administration and said that he joined "a long list of individuals who have come under attack from people inside and outside of the Clinton administration."[344] He added that "I have certainly made some mistakes that are mine and mine alone. There was a relationship many years ago from which a child was born. I am the father. With my wife's knowledge, I have fulfilled my responsibilities as the father."[345]

Burton said that he had always paid child support for the child who bore a different last name than his and lamented that the woman (who was now married) and her son had been subjected to inappropriate media scrutiny.

"I have apologized to my wife and family. I apologize to my constituents. We live in a society that rightfully depends upon people taking responsibility for their actions. I have done so in this matter," Burton said.[346]

With that, Burton shooed away TV reporters and others from the driveway of his home and, referring back to his statement, said, "I'm not going to talk anymore about my personal life. I've hurt some people that I love very much. Enough is enough."[347]

The political fallout was quick and ugly. While *Vanity Fair* abandoned its article written by Pulitzer Prize–winning journalist Russell Baker, the online publication *Salon* soon picked it up, expanding it to include serious questions about Burton's campaign fundraising tactics.

Salon spared no words, Baker's story noting that review of Burton's life revealed a portrait of "a Capitol Hill potentate who has apparently abused his power by using strong-arm and unethical campaign finance practices and by preying on female lobbyists, staffers and constituents."[348]

The disclosures mattered little; Burton rolled up the highest vote total of any person running for Congress in Indiana in 1998 (against a convicted felon whom the Indiana Democratic Party had sued to try and remove from the ballot). In the five elections that followed, Burton's electoral margins grew as he easily dispatched both Democratic and Independent opponents. In fact, he faced no serious electoral challenge for his seat until the May 2010 Republican primary, when he bested a competitive field of six GOP challengers and went on to win reelection to his fourteenth term in Congress.[349]

Notes

PART I: INFAMOUS CELEBRITIES

1. Smith, *Hoosiers in Hollywood*, 161.
2. *Life* magazine, January 26, 1942.
3. McCracken, *Las Vegas*, 50–51.
4. *Indianapolis Star*, January 17, 1942; McCracken, *Las Vegas*.
5. McCracken, *Las Vegas*, 50–51.
6. *Indianapolis Star*, January 17, 1942.
7. *Indianapolis Star*, January 18, 1942.
8. Smith, *Hoosiers in Hollywood*, 163.
9. Price, *Indiana Legends*, 123.
10. FBI Memo, Special Agent in Charge, Indianapolis to J. Edgar Hoover, Director, June 11, 1957, retrieved online at http://foia.fbi.gov/kinsey_alfred/kinsey_alfred_part01.pdf.
11. Ibid.
12. Ibid.
13. See Pomeroy, *Dr. Kinsey and the Institute*.
14. *Time* magazine, August 13, 1956.
15. Ibid.
16. Wells, *Being Lucky*, 186–87.
17. Pomeroy, *Dr. Kinsey and the Institute*, 325.

18. FBI memo, November 13, 1959.

19. *Los Angeles Times*, December 30, 2010.

20. *Indianapolis News*, January 9, 1962.

21. Ibid.

22. *Indianapolis Star*, November 15, 1961.

23. *New York Daily News*, January 14, 1943; *New York Times*, January 15, 1943.

24. *Indianapolis Star*, October 26, 1965.

25. *Indianapolis Star*, January 26, 1983.

26. *Indianapolis Star*, September 21, 1972.

27. *Indianapolis Star*, November 26, 1978.

28. Doll, *Elvis for Dummies*, 241.

29. Ibid., 240.

30. Ibid., 241.

31. Ibid., 240.

32. *Indianapolis Star*, June 27, 1977.

33. *Indianapolis News*, June 27, 1977.

34. Ibid.

35. Ibid.

36. See Kirchberg and Hendrickx, *Elvis Presley*.

37. *People* magazine, June 11, 2003.

38. Associated Press, May 22, 2003.

39. Associated Press, December 10, 2003.

40. *Sports Illustrated* magazine, February 10, 1992.

41. *Time* magazine, February 10, 1992.

42. *Time* magazine, February 24, 1992.

43. Ibid.

44. Associated Press, May 28, 2003.

45. *Indianapolis Star*, July 22, 1997.

46. See Farley and Colby, *Chris Farley Show*.

47. Ibid.

48. Ibid.

49. *Houston Chronicle*, October 28, 1997.

50. *Playboy* magazine interview, as reported in the *Wisconsin State Journal*, December 20, 1997.

51. Associated Press, December, 19, 1997.

52. *Los Angeles Times*, January 13, 1998.

53. Associated Press, January 3, 1998.
54. Ibid.
55. *Los Angeles Times*, August 27, 2005.
56. *Indianapolis Star*, December 19, 1999.

Part II: Infamous Criminals

57. *Indianapolis News*, September 6, 1933.
58. Ibid.
59. *Time* magazine, August 6, 1934.
60. *Indianapolis Star*, March 11, 1970.
61. Ibid.
62. Ibid.
63. Ibid.
64. *Indianapolis Star*, March 12, 1970.
65. *Time* magazine, February 21, 1977.
66. Ibid.
67. WISH-TV, Indianapolis, archival video February 1977, collection of the author.
68. Ibid.
69. Ibid.
70. Ibid.
71. Ibid.
72. Ibid.
73. Ibid.
74. *Indianapolis Star*, September 2, 1978.
75. *Indianapolis Star*, September 3, 1978.
76. Ibid.
77. *Indianapolis Star*, September 5, 1978.
78. *Indianapolis Star*, September 6, 1978.
79. *Indianapolis Star*, September 7, 1978.
80. *Indianapolis Star*, October 18, 1981.
81. *Indianapolis Star*, October 16, 1981.
82. Ibid.

83. *Indianapolis Star* Online Fact File, retrieved online at http://blogs.indystar. com/starfiles/2010/09/02/the_bomb_that_m.

84. *People* magazine, June 19, 1989.

85. Ibid.

86. Ibid.

87. Ibid.

88. Ibid.

89. Associated Press, July 30, 1989.

90. Associated Press, August 3, 1990.

91. Associated Press, April 18, 1991; U.S. Bureau of Prisons, Inmate Locator, retrieved online at http://www.bop.gov/iloc2/LocateInmate.jsp.

92. *Indianapolis Woman* magazine, April 2002.

93. Ibid.

94. PBS Broadcast, *Nova*, "The Bombing of America," originally broadcast on March 25, 1997. Transcript retrieved online at http://www.pbs.org/ wgbh/nova/transcripts/2310tbomb.html.

95. *Indianapolis News*, April 18, 1989.

96. *Indianapolis News*, April 19, 1989.

97. *Indianapolis News*, April 18, 1989.

98. Ibid.

99. *Indianapolis Woman* magazine, April 2002.

100. *Indianapolis Star*, April 25, 1990; *Nova*, "The Bombing of America."

101. *Indianapolis Star*, April 25, 1990.

102. Ibid.

103. Ibid.

104. *Indianapolis Woman* magazine, April 2002.

105. WTHR-TV, Indianapolis, May 11, 2009.

106. Ibid.

107. Ibid.

108. Ibid.

109. Lockwood, *Journal of Social Hygiene* 5, 587.

110. Barnes, *Amended Charter and Revised Ordinances*, 153–55.

111. W. Doherty, "Indianapolis Fire Department," in Bodenhamer and Barrows, *Encyclopedia of Indianapolis*, 775.

112. See Carter, *Reports of Cases Argued and Determined*.

113. Goethe, "Prevention of Venereal Diseases," 382–85.

114. Minutes of the Indiana State Medical Society, April 14, 1908, reported in the *Journal of the Indiana State Medical Association* 1.

115. See Clopper, "Night Messenger Service in Indiana."

116. Ibid.

117. Ibid.

118. E.V. Debs, "Never Be a Soldier," *Socialist Appeal*, August 28, 1915.

119. Sargent, "Eugene V. Debs Rescues a Modern Magdalene," 240.

120. Ibid.

121. *Journal of Social Hygiene* 3, 138–42.

122. Bogart, "Why Do Women Become Prostitutes?" 191–95.

123. R.J. Goldstein, "Pornographic Shows Spread in Midwest," *New York Times*, March 11, 1973. Found in *Political Censorship* (New York: Taylor & Francis, 2001).

124. Ibid.

125. See Cady, *Deadline Indianapolis.*

126. *Jet* magazine, "Indianapolis Court Convicts First Man for Prostitution," March 18, 1976.

127. Associated Press, May 14, 1990.

128. Ibid.

PART III: INFAMOUS DISASTERS

129. *Indianapolis News*, January 27, 1890.

130. Ibid.

131. *New York Times*, February 1, 1884.

132. *Indianapolis News*, January 27, 1890.

133. *Indianapolis Star*, October 28, 1903.

134. Ibid.

135. *Indianapolis Star*, November 1, 1903.

136. Associated Press, November 6, 1903.

137. Ibid.

138. *Indianapolis News*, November 5, 1903.

139. Associated Press, February 3, 1924.

140. *Anderson Daily Bulletin*, February 4, 1924.

141. Ibid.

142. Ibid.

143. *Anderson Daily Bulletin*, February 7, 1924.

144. *Indianapolis Star*, October 15, 1927.

145. *Indianapolis News*, October 15, 1927.

146. *Indianapolis Star*, October 15, 1927.

147. *Indianapolis News*, October 15, 1927.

148. *Indianapolis Star*, April 18, 1905.

149. Ibid.

150. Ibid.

151. Ibid.

152. Ibid.

153. Ibid.

154. Ibid.

155. *Indianapolis News*, April 18, 1905.

156. *Indianapolis Journal*, March 18, 1890.

157. Ibid.

158. *Indiana State Sentinel*, January 27, 1892.

159. *Indianapolis Journal*, January 22, 1892.

160. *Indiana State Sentinel*, January 27, 1892.

161. *Encyclopedia of Indianapolis*, 1994, 1,041.

162. *Indianapolis Journal*, May 21, 1888.

163. *New York Times*, April 18, 1904.

164. *Indiana Medical Journal* 22, 1904.

165. *Indianapolis Star*, June 7, 1908; *Indianapolis News*, June 6, 1908.

166. *Indianapolis Star*, January 31, 1958.

167. Ibid.

168. *Encyclopedia of Indianapolis*, 1994, 1,337.

169. *Indianapolis Times*, December 23, 1964.

170. Ibid.

171. *Indianapolis Star*, December 18, 1964.

172. Ibid.

173. *Shelbyville News*, December 18, 1964.

174. *Indianapolis Times*, December 20, 1964.

175. *Shelbyville News*, December 19, 1964.

176. Iezzoni, *1918*, 50.

177. *Indianapolis Star*, October 7, 1918.

178. *Indianapolis Star*, November 24, 1918.

179. Ibid.

180. *Indianapolis News*, November 19, 1918.

181. *Indianapolis Star*, November 24, 1918.

182. *Indianapolis Star*, November 26, 1918.

183. U.S. Bureau of Census, Monthly Statistics, 1919, 28–31.

184. Ritter Russo, *One Hundred Years*, 102.

185. *Indianapolis Times*, June 1, 1945.

186. Ibid.

187. *Time* magazine, June 11, 1945.

188. Ibid.

189. Ibid.

190. *Indianapolis News*, June 2, 1945.

191. *Indianapolis Times*, June 1, 1945.

192. Ibid.

193. Ibid.

194. *Indianapolis Times*, June 5, 1945.

195. *Indianapolis Star*, May 31, 1960.

196. *Indianapolis Star*, November 1, 1963.

197. Ibid.

198. *Indianapolis News*, November 2, 1963.

199. *Time* magazine, November 8, 1963.

200. *Indianapolis Times*, November 1, 1963.

201. *Indianapolis News*, December 9, 1963; *Indianapolis Times*, December 10, 1963; *Indianapolis Star*, December 10, 1963.

202. *Indianapolis Star* Online Fact File, retrieved online at http://www.indystar.com/article/99999999/NEWS06/80817011/StarFiles-1963-Coliseum-explosion.

203. See Drabek, *Disaster in Aisle 13*.

204. *Indianapolis Star*, September 10, 1969.

205. Ibid.

206. Ibid.

207. Ibid.

208. Ibid.

209. Ibid.

210. Ibid.

211. Ibid.

212. Ibid.

213. *Indianapolis Star*, September 11, 1969.

214. National Transportation Safety Board Report, U.S. Department of Transportation, Aircraft Accident Report File No. 1-0016, July 15, 1970.

215. Ibid.

216. Ibid.

217. United States Fire Administration, National Fire Data Center, Technical Report Series: "Ramada Inn Air Crash, Wayne Township, Indiana, October 20, 1987." Federal Emergency Management Agency.

218. *Indianapolis Star*, October 21, 1987.

219. United States Fire Administration, "Ramada Inn Air Crash."

220. *Indianapolis Star*, October 21, 1987.

221. United States Fire Administration, "Ramada Inn Air Crash."

222. Ibid.

223. *Indianapolis Monthly* magazine, September 1997.

224. Ibid.

225. *Chicago Sun-Times*, November 1, 1994.

226. *Chicago Sun-Times*, November 2, 1994.

227. *Chicago Sun-Times*, November 1, 1994.

228. *Chicago Sun-Times*, November 2, 1994.

229. *Indianapolis Star* Online Fact File, retrieved online at http://www.indystar.com/article/99999999/NEWS06/101028009/StarFiles-1994-Roselawn-plane-crash.

230. Associated Press, September 25, 2002.

231. Ibid.

232. Associated Press, May 24, 2001.

233. Ibid.

PART IV: INFAMOUS POLITICIANS

234. Moore, *Rebellion Record*, 64.

235. Ibid.

236. Ibid.

237. *Indianapolis Journal*, May 18, 1890.

238. *New York Times*, May 18, 1890.

239. *Indianapolis Journal*, May 18, 1890.

240. See Colbert in *Vice Presidents*.

241. Ibid.

242. Ibid., 206.

243. Ibid.

244. *Indianapolis Times*, January 5, 1948.

245. Ibid.

246. Ibid.

247. *Indianapolis Journal*, October 25, 1892.

248. Ibid.

249. *Indianapolis Times*, January 5, 1948.

250. *Indianapolis Journal*, April 5, 1896.

251. *Indianapolis Journal*, April 6, 1896.

252. *Indianapolis Times*, January 5, 1948.

253. *New York Times*, May 30, 1907.

254. Ibid.

255. Boomhower in *Vice Presidents*, 256–57.

256. Ibid.

257. *New York Times*, September 8, 1919.

258. Ibid.

259. *New York Times*, August 20, 1912.

260. Ibid.

261. Ibid.

262. Hartstad in *Vice Presidents*, 269.

263. *Indianapolis Star*, November 4, 1913; *Encyclopedia of Indianapolis*, 1994, 1,122.

264. *Indianapolis Star*, July 6, 1919.

265. Ibid.

266. *Indianapolis Star*, July 16, 1919.

267. Ibid.

268. Ibid.

269. *Indianapolis Star*, July 6, 1919.

270. Ibid.

271. *Indianapolis Star*, July 6, 1919; *Indianapolis News*, July 7, 1919.

272. *Indianapolis Star*, July 7, 1919.

273. *Indianapolis Star*, July 8, 1919.

274. Ibid.

275. See *Encyclopedia of Indianapolis*, 1994.

276. See Lutzholtz, *Grand Dragon*; see Tucker, *Dragon and the Cross*.

277. *Time* magazine, July 18, 1927.

278. Wade, *Fiery Cross*, 246.

279. Trimble in *Governors of Indiana*, 264.

280. Ibid., 265.

281. Ibid.

282. Lantzer in *Governors of Indiana*, 275.

283. Ibid., 278.

284. Walsh, *Centennial History*, 586.

285. Ibid., 586–87.

286. Ibid.

287. *Jet* magazine, March 12, 1953.

288. *Jet* magazine, January 29, 1959.

289. *Time* magazine, May 15, 1964; *Indiana Magazine of History*, March 1979.

290. *Time* magazine, April 24, 1964.

291. Ibid.

292. Ibid.

293. Ibid.

294. *Time* magazine, May 15, 1972.

295. Ibid.

296. Associated Press, July 1, 1986.

297. *New York Times*, July 1, 1986.

298. Walsh, *Centennial History*, 573.

299. Associated Press, July 1, 1986.

300. *Time* magazine, October 18, 1976.

301. Associated Press, February 3, 2008.

302. Associated Press, July 25, 1981.

303. *Indianapolis Star*, April 11, 1985.

304. Ibid.

305. *Indianapolis Star*, March 21, 1985.

306. *Indianapolis Star*, March 28, 1985, and April 2, 1985.

307. *Indianapolis Star*, April 2, 1985.

308. Ibid.

309. Associated Press, April 19, 1985.

310. *Indianapolis News*, December 7, 1995.

311. *New York Times*, August 20, 1988.

312. Video can likely be found online via YouTube, but see also the transcript of the Quayle-Bentsen debate at the Commission on Presidential Debates website, http://www.debates.org/index.php?page=october-5-1988-debate-transcripts.

313. *New York Times*, June 25, 1992.

314. Stephanopoulos, *All Too Human*, 9.

315. *Time* magazine, July 16, 1990.

316. Quayle, *Standing Firm*, 78.

317. *Indianapolis Monthly* magazine, June 1998.

318. *Indianapolis News*, December 11, 1989.

319. Ibid.

320. *Indianapolis News*, December 15, 1989.

321. Ibid.

322. Ibid.

323. Ibid.

324. *Indianapolis Star*, December 16, 1989.

325. *Indianapolis Monthly* magazine, June 1998.

326. Indiana Supreme Court, Disciplinary Commission, Case No. 49S00-9511-DI-1268, In the Matter of Dwayne M. Brown.

327. *Indianapolis News*, November 2, 1995.

328. Ibid.

329. Ibid.

330. Ibid.

331. *Indianapolis News*, December 5, 1995.

332. Ibid.

333. Ibid.

334. Ibid.

335. *Indianapolis News*, December 6, 1995.

336. Ibid.

337. Ibid.

338. Ibid.

339. *Indianapolis News*, December 7, 1995.

340. *People* magazine, April 4, 1994; WTHR-TV, Indianapolis, July 12, 2007.

341. Salon.com, December 22, 1998, retrieved online at http://www.salon.com/news/1998/12/cov_22newsa.html.

342. Ibid.

343. Ibid.

344. *Indianapolis Star*, September 5, 1998.

345. Ibid.

346. Ibid.

347. Ibid.

348. Salon.com, December 22, 1998, retrieved online at http://www.salon.com/news/1998/12/cov_22newsa.html.

349. Clerk, U.S. House of Representatives, Indiana Secretary of State, Elections Division.

Bibliography

Barnes, E. *Amended Charter and Revised Ordinances of the City of Indianapolis with the Rules of Order of the Common Council*. Indianapolis, IN: self-published, 1864.

Bayh, Birch. *One Heartbeat Away: Presidential Disability and Succession*. Indianapolis, IN: Bobbs-Merrill, 1968.

Bodenhamer, David J., and Robert G. Barrows. *The Encyclopedia of Indianapolis*. Bloomington: Indiana University Press, 1994.

Bogart, G.H. "Why Do Women Become Prostitutes?" *Medical Herald*. Vol. 35. Ann Arbor, MI: University of Michigan Press, 1916.

Boomhower, Ray E. "Charles Warren Fairbanks." *Vice Presidents: A Biographical Dictionary*. 4th ed. Edited by L. Edward Purcell. New York: Infobase Publishing, 2009.

Cady, Dick. *Deadline Indianapolis: The Story Behind the Stories at the Pulliam Press*. Indianapolis, IN: Riverview Books, LLC, 2010.

Calhoun, Charles W. *Benjamin Harrison*. New York: Henry Holt, 2005.

Bibliography

Carter, Dan T. *The Politics of Rage: George Wallace, the Origins of New Conservatism, and the Transformation of American Politics.* Baton Rouge, LA: LSU Press, 2000.

Carter, H.E. *Reports of Cases Argued and Determined in the Supreme Court of Judicature of the State of Indiana.* Vol. 22. Indianapolis, IN: Bobbs-Merrill Company, 1864.

Cavinder, Fred D. *Historic Indianapolis Crimes: Murder and Mystery in the Circle City.* Charleston, SC: The History Press, 2010.

Clopper, E.N. "The Night Messenger Service in Indiana." Report of the Rational Child Labor Committee to the Indiana Child Labor Commission. *Public Welfare in Indiana*, Issues 84–91. Indianapolis: Indiana Department of Public Welfare, 1911.

Colbert, Thomas B. "Thomas A. Hendricks." *Vice Presidents: A Biographical Dictionary.* 4th ed. Edited by L. Edward Purcell. New York: Infobase Publishing, 2009.

Cromie, Robert, and Joseph Pinkston. *Dillinger: A Short and Violent Life.* Ann Arbor: University of Michigan Press, 1962.

Davidson, Donald, and Rick Shaffer. *Autocourse: Official History of the Indianapolis 500.* Norwalk, CT: MBI Publishing Company, 2006.

Doll, Susan. *Elvis for Dummies.* Indianapolis, IN: Wiley Publishing, Inc., 2009.

Drabek, Thomas E. *Disaster in Aisle 13: A Case Study of the Coliseum Explosion at the Indiana State Fairgrounds, Oct. 31, 1963.* Columbus: Ohio State University Press, 1968.

Farley, Thomas, Jr., and Tanner Colby. *The Chris Farley Show: A Biography in Three Acts.* New York: Penguin, 2009.

Frady, Marshall. *Wallace: The Classic Portrait of Alabama Governor George C. Wallace.* New York: Random House, 2009.

Gathorne-Hardy, Jonathan. *Sex and the Measure of All Things: A Life of Alfred C. Kinsey.* Bloomington: Indiana University Press, 1998.

Goethe, L. "The Prevention of Venereal Diseases." *Journal of the Indiana State Medical Association* 1 (1908): 382–85.

Greasley, Philip A., and the Society for the Study of Midwestern Literature. *Dictionary of Midwestern Literature: The Authors.* Bloomington: Indiana University Press, 2001.

Harstad, Peter T. "Thomas Riley Marshall." *Vice Presidents: A Biographical Dictionary.* 4th ed. Edited by L. Edward Purcell. New York: Infobase Publishing, 2009.

Harvey, Paul, and Philip Goff. *The Columbia Documentary History of Religion in America Since 1945.* New York: Routledge, 2005.

Iezzoni, Lynette. *1918: The Worst Epidemic in American History.* New York: TV Books, LLC, 1999.

Indiana Medical Journal Publishing Company. *Indiana Medical Journal: A Monthly Journal of Medicine and Surgery.* Vol. 22. Indianapolis: Indiana Medical Journal Publishing Company, 1904.

Kinsey, Alfred C., Wardell B. Pomeroy and Clyde E. Martin. *Sexual Behavior in the Human Male.* Bloomington: Indiana University Press, 1948.

Kinsey, Alfred C., Wardell B. Pomeroy, Clyde E. Martin, Paul H. Gebhard and staff of the Institute for Sexual Research, Indiana University. *Sexual Behavior in the Human Female.* Bloomington: Indiana University Press, 1953.

Kirchberg, Connie, and Marc Hendrickx. *Elvis Presley, Richard Nixon and the American Dream.* Jefferson, NC: McFarland and Company, 1999.

Kramer, Ralph. *Indianapolis 500: A Century of Excitement.* Iolla, WI: Krause Publications, 2010.

Kriebel, Robert C. *Ross Ade: Their Purdue Stories, Stadiums and Legacies.* West Lafayette, IN: Purdue University Press, 2009.

Lantzer, Jason S. "Edward L. Jackson, January 12, 1925–January 14, 1929." *The Governors of Indiana.* Edited by Linda G. Gugin and James E. St. Clair. Indianapolis: Indiana Historical Society Press, 2006.

Lockwood, V.H. *Journal of Social Hygiene* 5 (1919): 587. Publication of the American Social Hygiene Association. Stanford, University of California Press.

Lutzholtz, M. William. *Grand Dragon: D.C. Stephenson and the Ku Klux Klan in Indiana.* West Lafayette, IN: Purdue University Press, 1991.

Mark, David. *Going Dirty: The Art of Negative Campaigning.* Lanham, MD: Rowman & Littlefield Publishers, Inc., 2006.

McCracken, Robert D. *Las Vegas: The Great American Playground.* Portland, OR: Marion Street Press, 1996.

Moore, Frank, ed. *The Rebellion Record: A Diary of American Events with Documents, Narratives, Illustrations, Incidents, and Poetry.* Vol. 4. Boston, MA: Harvard University Press, 1862.

Pomeroy, Wardell B. *Dr. Kinsey and the Institute for Sex Research.* New Haven, CT: Yale University Press, 1982.

Price, Nelson A. *Indiana Legends: Famous Hoosiers from Johnny Appleseed to David Letterman.* Indianapolis, IN: Emmis Books, 1997.

Profeta, Louis M. *The Patient in Room Nine Says He's God.* Winchester, UK: O Books, 2010.

Quayle, Dan. *Standing Firm: A Vice Presidential Memoir.* New York: Harper Collins, 1994.

Reiterman, Timothy, and John Jacobs. *Raven: The Untold of the Reverend Jim Jones and His People.* New York: Penguin, 2008.

Ritter Russo, Dorothy, ed., with Charles N. Combs and Edgar F. Kiser. *One Hundred Years of Indiana Medicine, 1849–1949.* Indianapolis: Indiana State Medical Association, 1949.

Sargent, J.S. "Eugene V. Debs Rescues a Modern Magdalene." *Flaming Sward.* Vol. 27. Ann Arbor: MI: University of Michigan Press and Guiding Star, 1913.

Singer, Mark. *Citizen K: The Deeply Weird American Journey of Brett Kimberlin.* New York: Knopf, 1996.

Smith, David L. *Hoosiers in Hollywood.* Indianapolis: Indiana Historical Society, 2006.

Stephanopoulos, George. *All Too Human: A Political Education.* New York: Little, Brown & Company, 1999.

Stoner, Andrew E. *Notorious 92: The Most Infamous Murder from Each of Indiana's 92 Counties.* Indianapolis, IN: Blue River Press, 2009.

Trimble, Tony L. "Warren T. McCray, January 10, 1921–April 30, 1924." *The Governors of Indiana.* Edited by Linda G. Gugin and James E. St. Clair. Indianapolis: Indiana Historical Society Press, 2006.

Tucker, Richard K. *The Dragon and the Cross: The Rise and Fall of the Ku Klux Klan in Middle America.* Hamden, CT: Archon Books, 1991.

Wade, Wyn Craig. *The Fiery Cross of the Ku Klux Klan in America.* New York: Oxford University Press, 1998.

BIBLIOGRAPHY

Walsh, Justin E. *The Centennial History of the Indiana General Assembly, 1816–1978.* Indianapolis: Select Committee on the Centennial History of the Indiana General Assembly and the Indiana Historical Bureau, 1987.

Wells, Herman B. *Being Lucky: Reminiscences and Reflections.* Bloomington: Indiana University Press, 1980.

About the Author

A ndrew E. Stoner (born 1964) is a native of Goshen, Indiana, and lived in Indianapolis for twenty-six years. He started writing as a boy by teaching himself to type on an old Underwood manual typewriter. A journalist by training, his writing has been published in the *South Bend Tribune*, the *Goshen News*, the *Indianapolis Star*, the *Indianapolis Recorder*, *Sports Illustrated* and *Colliers Worldbook Encyclopedia*. He holds a bachelor's degree in journalism from Franklin College of Indiana and a master's degree in journalism from Ball State University. He is currently completing a PhD in journalism and technical communications at Colorado State University, Fort Collins, Colorado.

Also by Andrew E. Stoner:

Notorious 92: The Most Infamous Murder From Each of Indiana's 92 Counties
Legacy of a Governor: The Life of Indiana's Frank O'Bannon
Those '70s Shows